TOM

Thomas Coryell

ISBN 978-1-64003-070-1 (Paperback)
ISBN 978-1-64003-071-8 (Digital)

Copyright © 2017 Thomas Coryell
All rights reserved
First Edition

All rights reserved. No part of this publication may be reproduced, distributed, or transmitted in any form or by any means, including photocopying, recording, or other electronic or mechanical methods without the prior written permission of the publisher. For permission requests, solicit the publisher via the address below.

Covenant Books, Inc.
11661 Hwy 707
Murrells Inlet, SC 29576
www.covenantbooks.com

Introduction

Is LIFE BY design? Do things happen on purpose? Could it be that the events happening all around us, and the people who cross our path every day, are intentional? Is there a plan for it all?

For those of us with spiritual faith, those answers are easy. Believing in a higher power, and in divine intervention, is a core value to a vast number of people all around the world. It often helps us answer the hard questions that come with the toughest of things that life can throw at us. One of those tough questions is *why?* Why do bad things happen? Why do they happen to good people?

The answer to why is vague at best, even for those with deep, religious convictions. Casting off those worries to a higher power is not easy. There is an inherent need for people to understand and make sense of it all. Often, the answer never comes. People pass from this life having never received clarity on that certain something.

- What if that tragedy had never occurred?
- What if I had never met that person?
- How different would my life be?

But sometimes we *are* blessed with such answers. Perhaps in a strange dream, or in a bizarre set of coincidences. Years, or even decades later, a nugget of truth comes to light, and we experience a full-circle moment. In those moments of epiphany, we realize something—life actually *is* by design. That certain something really *did* have meaning, and it was special. It served a purpose far greater than my own grief, way more important than my personal loss. God's work *was* done that day. Wow!

CHAPTER ONE

The Early Years

It was a typical, warm summer day in Pekin, Illinois, on July 22, 1956. A little boy was outside playing in the dirt to the sound of his own gunfire and Indian war cry sound effects. A battle raged between his tiny cowboys and Indians figures. A man approached and stood there silently for a moment. The boy looked up at the stranger.

Man: "Are you Tommy?"

Boy: "Yes."

Man: "You're having a birthday today, aren't you?"

Boy (exclaiming with the happy smile of a birthday boy): "Yes!"

Man: "Well, I'm your dad."

As Tom shares that story, he recalls, "I'd like to think I got really emotional and all, but you know something, it didn't even dawn on me what a dad was. Because I never had one."

It is true that John Daniel was Tom's biological father, but John was never really a dad to Tom. At age fifty-something, Tom had learned some interesting truths about his father while at a family reunion. John's younger brother, Otho, was there at the reunion. Tom took that opportunity to ask Otho what he knew about his mom and dad and what happened to them. Otho told him a sad story about his own father, Arthur Elmer.

Arthur was a mechanic in the late 1920s. He had no garage, so he worked on vehicles out in the yard. On a particularly cold and wet December day, he spent several hours on the job out in the elements. He contracted double pneumonia from the exposure. Since health care was not so great in those days, there weren't many treatments available for Arthur. He passed away on Christmas Day, December 25, 1930, at the age of forty-three.

Arthur left behind a wife, Efelda, and six children—Ruth, Otho, Edyth, Babe, Kenneth, and John Daniel (Tom's father). Efelda had no means to support the kids or to keep the business going. There was no savings and no insurance. All she could do was sell off the family home and whatever else she had of value to try and make ends meet. Like millions of other families all across America suffering under the Great Depression, Efelda ran out of money and out of options. The kids had to go elsewhere to be cared for.

John and his older brother Babe ended up in Wyoming working as ranch hands. That's where John spent his teenage years, falling in love with cowboy country and the ranch life. But that's not the only thing John fell in love with. He got himself involved with the ranch owner's daughter, Ellinor. But she was already married with children. The affair turned into an ugly situation when they were discovered. It resulted in John and Babe getting kicked off the ranch. There was a World War gearing up at the time, so the boys enlisted. John went into the Air Force, called the Army Air Corps at the time.

Some years later, John ended up in Ohio working as a pipe fitter. That's where he met and married another woman with the same name, spelled slightly different—Elinor. In less than three years, John and Elinor had four children together: Carol came first in December 1943; then came the twins, Timothy and Tilden, in March 1945; then Thomas Dean in July 1946. During those years, building a life with Elinor, John never stopped thinking about the true love of his life back on the ranch in Wyoming. On the very day of Tom's birth,

TOM

July 22, 1946, John received word from Wyoming that the "other" Ellinor had lost her husband in an accident. John did the unthinkable. He ran away to Wyoming, abandoning his wife in the hospital laboring in delivery.

Over the next ten years, John made rare visits to the kids for birthdays or other occasions.

Tom recalls, "I have no lasting memory of him until that day he talked to me about my birthday. I remember being scared whenever he came around. One time I remember running to my room to hide in the closet. I remember he got real mad and yelled at my mom and grandma and left."

Looking back through the eyes of an adult, Tom realizes that John was never a welcome guest by anyone after what he had done to Elinor. It was a very awkward and tense time whenever he darkened their doorstep.

On that summer day in 1956, John stood there and told a son he'd never known that he wanted to buy him a birthday present.

John: "Do you like to catch fish?"

Tommy: "Yes."

John: "Would you like to have a spin-cast outfit or a rod and reel?"

Tommy (knowing that spin-cast was the newest thing out, and anybody who was somebody had one): "I want a spin-cast!"

John: "Okay then! I'll see you later."

Tommy was so excited! He dared not leave the house in case that guy came back with the spin-cast. He stayed put, playing with his cowboys and Indians. He went in for dinner then went right back out. He waited and watched, and waited some more. He waited until it was dark.

In his owns words, Tom recalls, "He never showed up. I never saw my dad again until I was out of high school. I never got the rod and reel, but believe me, I was out there, totally excited and waiting to get that spin-cast. It meant more to me than even knowing he was my dad."

There is more sadness to Tom's childhood story that resulted from John Daniel running off to Wyoming. While still in the hospital recovering from the labor of delivering Tom into the world, the news had come to Elinor about what John had done. Understandably, Elinor was livid. She flew into a rage, which was likely enhanced by the hormonal imbalance that was in her body from the pregnancy.

In 1946, mental health treatment was a joke by twenty-first-century standards. Doctors and nurses had no clue how to deal with the emotional trauma that Elinor was experiencing, so they treated her like a mental patient. She was considered crazy and was eventually committed to Bartonville Mental Hospital. They locked her away in a padded room, pumped her full of sedatives, and restrained her with a straitjacket. That's no joke. That's serious incarceration.

The four children ended up with Elinor's mother, Flossie. Flossie and her husband, Leland, owned a large house on Park Avenue in Pekin at the time, which operated as a nursing home. That became the childhood home for Tom, Carol, Tim, and Til.

For years, Flossie took advantage of Elinor's situation, taking steps to keep her in the system as she collected state aid on the four kids, aid that was fraudulently redirected into the nursing home business and for Flossie's personal use.

Tom recalls, "Me and my sister always believed she wasn't crazy. She was just very mad. She would slip notes to Carol, begging her to find her friend Irene and tell her where she was at . . . that she was not crazy. But my grandmother found those notes, and Irene never knew what was happening to her friend."

Some years later, Elinor was finally released from Bartonville and came to live at the nursing home. Flossie conscripted her own daughter for labor, forcing her to work long hours of dirty work in exchange for room and board, and to repay the debt of raising her kids. Elinor was never the same person after those events.

Life was very strict for Tom and his siblings growing up in the nursing home. They received a single pair of pants and shoes to last all year long. They were only allowed to wear them to church or school, then had to immediately change into their old, holey ones afterward. There was no motherly or fatherly love, only occasional care and attention from overworked grandparents wrapped up in the daily schedule of a commercial operation. Tom acknowledges that the experience of growing up that way—never knowing his father, with an emotionally traumatized mother, and disconnected grandparents—had a profound effect on him.

He says, "I think I missed out on something very important with my own children by not knowing what it meant to be a dad."

There was a positive outcome from it for Tom. He learned at a very young age that no one was going to give him anything. He learned how to earn money for himself. He learned about hard work and how to win over his customers, which became lifelong character traits. Those traits have proven to be some critical success factors throughout Tom's adult life.

Tom remembers his first customer: "The first job I ever got was across the road with the principal of the grade school I was attending. I started mowing his lawn for $1.50. The person next to him hired me to do his lawn for 75 cents. It was a smaller yard. And then the person behind us let me do his yard for 50 cents. I ended up with 8 lawns that summer that I mowed every other week!"

Tom sold his labor services for all kinds of odd jobs—raking leaves in the fall, shoveling snow in the winter, painting fences, trimming hedges and bushes, cleaning up garages and basements.

Tom recalls with a big smile, "I was making money! I stuffed my wallet full of $1 bills so whenever I bought a soda or something, everyone could see my fat wallet!"

He improved his own life with the money he earned. He bought his own clothes—not just Levi's jeans, but *corduroy* Levi's jeans.

Tom laughs out loud as he recalls, "You had to be 'uptown' to wear corduroy Levi's! They were $6 a pair!"

He wore nice shoes, treated himself to burgers and shakes, and he was able to buy himself the toys he wanted; life was okay for Tommy growing up in that small Illinois farm town.

Chapter Two

High School Days

EVEN THOUGH TOM was involved in a church growing up, he had not yet fully experienced the call of Christ in his heart. In the summer of 1962, he was just a young man of sixteen, in between his freshman and sophomore years. The church was planning a field trip that summer to Chicago to experience the Billy Grahm Crusade. Flossie and Leland were chaperones for the event, so it was only natural that Tommy went along.

Tom remembers the day, "We had a pretty good spot up front, only about six rows back, so I had a really nice view of Billy Grahm. When he spoke, I felt a strange thing. It was as if Billy was speaking directly to me."

While the other guys were goofing around passing notes and not even listening, Tom focused on Billy's every word. The salvation message played strong upon Tom's heart like never before. When the time came for the invitation, something stirred inside him so bad that he was shaking and on the verge of crying. Some of the other guys around him sensed Tom's distress and tried to talk him out of it, but he felt a tap on the shoulder and turned to see his grandma Flossie.

"Do you want to go down there?" she asked.

"Yes," he replied.

Tom recalls the moment, "I went down there, and I accepted Christ. Everything changed for me that day. From then, until now as an old man, my life was different."

Tom had a very close friend named Scott during his teen years. Scott's father, Bud, took a strong liking to Tom and took the boys out hunting on several occasions for ducks, squirrels, and rabbits. He hired Tom for some part-time, cleanup work on his aluminum siding business and was quite impressed with the kid's ability to work so hard. Bud became the closest thing Tom ever had to a dad, guiding and mentoring him in those times. Tom recalls to this day some of the best advice that man ever gave to him.

"If you want to be successful in life, Tom, you surround yourself with successful, wealthy people, and you stay far away from the lazy ones," said Bud.

That advice has stayed with Tom his entire life, and he still follows that principle today.

At age fifteen, Tom acquired his work permit and took a summer job with Ace Spray General Service. That was his first introduction to pest control and lawn service on a commercial scale, and it became an invaluable experience for him later in life. For seventy-five cents an hour, Tom performed foundation whitewashes, applied chlordane treatments, and laid sod. He worked other jobs during his teen years and continued to do quite well, earning plenty of money and enjoying the rewards of his labor. When Tom was about age sixteen, his grandparents bought a cabin down at Spring Lake. He spent as much time there as he could, fishing, swimming, and hunting ducks. But there was another reason he went there so often. It was a girl.

Tom says, "That was probably the best thing to happen to us kids living down there. Also, that's where I met Pat, my first love. My grandma thought I really loved Spring Lake, but it wasn't the only reason I went down there so much!"

Over time, the two young lovebirds drifted apart for other interests. There were hundreds of other handsome boys and pretty girls. For Tom, there was also sports! He loved them all and found himself trying out for just about every sport the school offered.

TOM

In his own words, "I enjoyed sports immensely. I don't think there was anything I didn't try—wrestling, football, basketball, baseball, tennis, racquetball, handball."

As much as Tom loved football, he did not possess the size and strength to be very successful at it. Weighing barely 160, being a roving linebacker on a monster defense was quite the challenge. He was an underclassman junior as well, so he was stuck on second string and rarely got to play. Tired of watching from the sidelines, or stuck playing for the JV squad, Tom decided to try his skills as a kicker.

Tom recalls, "Every night after practice, I stayed out there until my leg was so sore I could hardly walk—kicking and kicking and kicking. This went on and on and on."

The hard work finally paid off for Tom when a senior captain noticed how good Tom was. He was consistently placing field goals between the uprights from forty-five yards out and launching punts as far as sixty yards. It was very clear to the team captain that they had the wrong guy kicking the ball, so they gave Tom a shot at the starting job in one of their most important home games of the season. Tom delivered, helping the team win that game and earned himself a starting position on the varsity team.

Tom learned a valuable life lesson as a young man with the basketball team. He had earned a spot on the team, surviving the dreaded cut. However, he was not quite as good a player as many others and ended up spending more time on the bench than he ever played. The coach even assigned him as the water boy. That didn't settle well with the prideful youth. Believing that he was better than that, he caved to his pride and quit the team.

Tom recalls, "Little did I know that the team I was on ended up winning the Midstate 8 Championship that year. That really irked me because I could have been in uniform in the very picture that graces the halls of Pekin High to this day for that championship team. Rats!"

Chapter Three

Love Blossoms

The Pekin school district was so populated that they had to build a second campus just for juniors and seniors. That was the baby boomer generation in 1962. Tom's sophomore class had over six hundred students. Rows and rows of lockers stretched the entire length of every hallway, alphabetized by student last name. Tom's locker was right next to a freshman girl named Isabelle. Their fates were sealed. As locker pals, they formed a fun friendship. Whenever they would see each other coming down the hallway toward each other, they would make a run for it, slide into each other, and bounce off their hips and shoulders. Tom never realized that Isabelle liked him for more than just a locker friend, but he found out rather quickly the next school year when he asked another girl to the junior prom.

Tom says, "She never did forgive me! Years later, even when we were married, she would always tell people, 'He never even asked me to the prom!' But I had no idea. I just thought we were friends."

The two began dating. As fate would have it, they both landed part-time jobs at the same grocery store. They took their breaks together and smooched in the back room. He walked her home after their shift and sat together on the porch, smooching some more. Their love grew, and on a particularly nice summer day, the couple decided to go on a real date.

TOM

There was a swimming place in the nearby town of Galesburg that Isabelle knew of. That was about an hour's drive away from Pekin. Tom had no car, so he made arrangements to borrow his brother's '57 Chevy. Off they went with a classic wicker-style picnic basket full of fried chicken and potato salad that Isabelle and her mother, Bobbye, had prepared, along with a red-and-white checkered cloth—like a picture postcard.

Tom reminisces with a soft smile on his face, "Those kinds of cloths still remind me of that day."

They swam, they ate, they laughed, and shared an amazing day together.

Tom recalls with a laugh, "She wore that yellow bikini, and she shouldn't have. Way too much skin coming in contact in the water. I lost control, and she got pregnant that day. It was my first date, the very first time I had the car to myself, the first time I ever went out to a picnic, the first time I ever kissed a girl like that, the first time I had sex, and she gets pregnant! Boy! I couldn't get away with nothing!"

It was a couple months after that picnic adventure when Tom and Isabelle began to realize they were in trouble. She had missed a couple of cycles. Not quite sure what to do, Tom and Isabelle went to his grandmother Flossie for some advice. That was a bad idea.

Flossie became very angry and told Tom, "You do *not* have to marry her just because you got her pregnant!"

Flossie tried to manipulate the situation and drive the two apart. She sent Tom away to Michigan to stay with her daughter Rosetta and told Tom to stay away from Isabelle. Before the summer was over, a letter came in the mail to Tom. It was from Isabelle. She asked him to please come back and speak with her father. She was three months along. He was beside himself. He didn't know what to do.

His aunt Rosetta would not advise him, saying, "This is on your conscience, Tom. You're going to have to decide for yourself."

He asked Rosetta to pray with him. As they prayed together, and he wrestled with his conscience, something clicked in his soul. Maybe it was the realization that he was about to banish an innocent child to the same fatherless life he had grown up in. Maybe it was the Spirit moving in answer to Tom and Rosetta's prayers.

Whatever it was, Tom recalls those events with disdain. "My grandmother wanted me to skip out and take off, to abandon the whole scene. I couldn't do that. In fact, I was a little bit upset. I told her that the child is mine, she's going to have my baby, and it's just as much my fault as it is hers. She yelled at me, 'How do you know it's yours, Tom!' I just know, Grandma," said Tom.

Flossie relented and allowed him to deal with the problem on his own. Now for Isabelle's parents, oh boy.

At six feet five inches tall, her dad, Thomas, was an imposing figure of a man. Barely six feet on his tippy-toes, Tom always felt small in the man's presence. It was especially uncomfortable that day as he sat there across the table waiting for him to start the conversation. He was reading a hardbound book, gliding his large hand back and forth across the pages while Tom sat in silence. It was probably less than a minute, but time seemed to slow to a crawl as Tom waited, and waited. He stared down at the table, and his mind began to drift, rehearsing the speech in his head over and over again, wondering what this large man was about to do to him. Tom wanted to make a good impression with Thomas and ask for his daughter's hand in marriage properly.

All of a sudden, he hastily closed the book with a loud *clap!* Tom jumped at the sound, visibly startled, and he felt an instant surge of anxiety. The exchange went something like this:

> Thomas (holding back an ornery grin, he put on his best fatherly countenance and bellowed in a deep voice): "Do you have something you want to tell me?"

> Tom (all of his preparations for that moment evaporated instantly as he was immediately reduced to the seventeen-year-old boy he truly was, seated there in front of a man whose daughter he had messed around with . . . geez. He began to stutter): "Sir, I came here to ask for your hand . . . for your marriage, for the hand . . . can I marry your daughter?"

TOM

> Thomas (looking down at the table and rubbing his forehead, he wasn't sure whether to laugh out loud or walk away): "Well, the cart is a bit before the horse here, isn't it?"
>
> Tom: "What do you mean?"
>
> Thomas: "You want to marry my daughter, but I think you kind of already did, didn't you?"

Tom recalls the moment, saying, "I didn't know what to say to the man. I was just a kid without wisdom. I couldn't have been more ashamed at that moment. I didn't want to mess up my life. I had plans to go into the Air Force, but there I was."

The conversation continued.

> Thomas: "Here's what you're going to have to do. You're going to quit school. You're going to get a full-time job, and you're going to show me that you're making $100 a week. I want to see your paycheck. When you're making $100 a week consistently and have a good job, then you can marry my daughter."
>
> Tom (sat there for a moment, processing. It didn't set well with him. It didn't sound right): "Sir, if I quit school now, there's no doubt in my mind I can make $100 a week. But that's all I'll ever make for rest of my life . . . for your daughter's life. If I can just finish one more year, I'll graduate, then I can give her a good life. We'll struggle for one year, not our whole life."
>
> Thomas (a big smile filled his face): "Well, hell yes, you can marry my daughter!"

At that moment, Tom realized he was being tested. The man apparently wanted to see what kind of character the kid had, and clearly, he was pleased with the outcome. So much so that he helped the young couple find their first home and even paid the rent.

On September 26, 1964, Tom and Isabelle were married. It was a small, informal church wedding, where the two were required to dress in nondescript clothing—no tuxedo, no white dress—as if to punish the kids for their premarital mistake.

Tom says, "We always regretted not ever having a real wedding, with her in a white dress."

Tom stayed in school and continued to work the supermarket job earning a meager $37.50 per week, but he made ends meet and paid the bills. He had no car and walked most everywhere. On May 15, 1965, Daniel Dean was born at Pekin Memorial Hospital. A few weeks later, despite his employer refusing to let him off work to attend commencement, the first father to ever graduate Pekin High School without dropping out had earned his diploma.

Times were tough for the young family, but they were together. There was health and happiness, with an ample supply of love and support from family, friends, and from each other. Life was good.

CHAPTER FOUR

Just Getting Started

IN JUNE OF 1965, Tom was enjoying his new life as a husband, father, and Pekin Class of '65 graduate, but something was missing. As he held little Daniel close, looked into his eyes, and felt a father-son love bond, he began to realize what it was—John Daniel, that guy who never came back with his fishing pole.

Being a father himself now, Tom couldn't help but wonder about this thing he had never known. He wanted to know who his dad was. At the time, Tom was also feeling a need to get away from the sleepy little Illinois farm town he had always known. He was about to turn eighteen and was ready for a change, so he contacted his aunt Edythe, John's sister, who was also living in Pekin at the time. Tom learned from her that John was living in Colorado Springs.

When he expressed his interest to Edythe in getting to know his dad, she replied, "He would really like to know that. I will contact him and then let him contact you, okay?"

Tom agreed. Several days later, he received a letter in the mail from John. Over the next couple of weeks, they wrote back and forth sharing the usual pleasantries that two strangers might exchange.

Tom chuckles as he recalls, "We didn't have text machines back then. We had to wait for the mail! I didn't have a phone either."

Eventually, they connected on the phone at Edythe's house to discuss the subject of Tom moving to Colorado.

John asked, "If I come out there with a U-Haul on Monday, will you be ready to pack up and move? I'm not coming all that way if you're going to change your mind."

Tom assured him that he fully intended to move with or without John's help. Monday came, and he was ready. As he anxiously watched out the front window of his tiny, upstairs apartment, sure enough, a station wagon pulled up alongside the curb towing a U-Haul trailer. John stepped out of the car, along with the "other" Ellinor.

"I think my dad's here," Tom said to Isabelle.

They headed downstairs to greet their visitors. They stood on the porch, Isabelle holding little Danny.

Tom describes the scene, "Isabelle was a very beautiful woman. The older she got, the prettier she got. By the time my dad got there, she was about as pretty as she could get. When he came to that porch, he looked up and saw Isabelle holding Danny. He walked right past me without even a look and gave Isabelle a big hug. He looked at Danny, then turned to me to say, 'Man, Tommy! You are one lucky guy! You got any coffee for your old man?' He turned and walked up the stairs. I never even got a handshake from that man."

They shared a pot of coffee and visited, making plans for the next day.

Tom remembers the occasion, saying, "He did most of the talking. He asked about me playing football and if I was still sure about moving. He talked about the long drive to Colorado and held Danny. He talked mostly to Isabelle. I remember sitting there feeling disappointed. I never knew my dad, and he seemed more interested in my wife and kid than me."

They spent a couple hours packing and loading the U-Haul. Young and poor, the two didn't have much to load, so the five-by-eight trailer was loaded quickly and had more than enough room for their things. John and Ellinor left for their hotel room, leaving the trailer behind. They finished the last bit of loading early the next morning, beds and such, and set out on the road to Colorado Springs.

For the next few weeks, they stayed at John and Ellinor's place. Tom was still without a car, so it was fortunate that he found a job at the same place where a neighbor girl also worked. He rode with her to his new job as a night watchman at the Emerson Electric Company. He started saving up for his own apartment and car.

During that time, Tom and John shared many conversations, telling stories and sipping whiskey (sometimes a little too much whiskey, Tom recalls). John learned about Tom's outdoor adventures at Spring Lake, so he knew there was a common interest between them in the shooting sports. July 22 arrived, Tom's birthday.

John said to Tom, "I'd like to get you something for your birthday."

The skeptical "okay" response from Tom carried certain undertones from years before that flew right over John's head.

John took him to a local gun shop that also operated as an Isaac Walton shooting club. John was a member, so he knew the right people there to help him set up the perfect .30–06 rifle. He picked out a decent, well-used model, selected a beautiful new scope for it, and proceeded to describe his exact specifications to the gunsmith on how he wanted the old gun restored to like-new condition for Tom.

John realized it would be some time before the rifle would be ready, so when they got back to the house, he decided to give Tom something that he could have that day. He handed Tom an old pocket watch he had owned for many years. John described it with pride, telling Tom how he had bought it long ago when he was a young man and that it would be one hundred years old in just fifteen more years. It was a classic Hamilton, no longer in business, with hand-etched markings inside that represented its maintenance record.

Tom recalls with a giggle, "It was one of those old-fashioned watch fobs. I had never worn a watch fob in my life. He bought me some house slippers too. I guess he wanted me to be a man like him, but it wasn't cool for a guy like me to wear a watch fob and slippers. I was only eighteen years old! But I said 'okay' and didn't complain."

Time went by. Tom and Isabelle got their own place and moved out. Then John called one day. The rifle was finally ready. As they stood there in the shop together examining the rifle, both were amazed at the quality craftsmanship. Tom admired the perfectly balanced feel of it in his hands and the butter-smooth operation of the bolt action.

"What a beautiful .30–06," he said.

They went back to John's house where his father proceeded to place the rifle in his own gun cabinet and locked it up.

"We'll take it to the range next weekend and get it sighted in," said John.

Not quite sure what to think of that, Tom simply shrugged his shoulders and said, "Okay."

The weekend came, and they went out to the range. Like an experienced pro, Tom got the rifle perfectly zeroed in at one hundred yards. When they were done with the rifle, John brought out a German Luger pistol. They moved up to fifty yards and set up a gallon jug on the berm. John was apparently going to teach Tom how to shoot a handgun. He demonstrated how to handle the old Luger, the proper way to hold it, and how to operate the action. John proceeded to fire. He fired, and fired, and fired, hitting all around the jug but never once did he actually hit it. Flustered, the man handed the gun to Tom, who immediately took five shots and nailed the jug five times.

"All right, all right! That's enough," said John.

He took the gun back and began packing up his gear. He was clearly done shooting. The drive back to John's place was awkwardly silent.

Tom recalls, "He never said 'good shooting' or nothing. He just took the gun and put it away. Personally, I think he was mad that I could hit that jug and he couldn't. He just didn't seem happy that I could do that."

It was late in the day by the time they got back.

Tom said, "I'd better be getting home."

John quickly responded rather rudely, "Oh no, you're not! We're not done! You shot those guns, and now they're dirty. You don't ever put your guns away dirty. You're gonna have to learn that right now, boy!"

Surprised at the attitude, Tom complied and spent the next hour doing a full fieldstrip, clean and oil, on the two guns.

TOM

Tom describes what happened next with a disgusted look on his face. "We get it all done, he stands up, takes the rifle, puts it in his cabinet, shuts the door, and locks it. Folks, I'm seventy years old, and I never did get that gun. If I ever wanted to use it, I had to go with him to his shooting club, bring it back, clean it, and put it right back in his cabinet. That gun was never mine."

After sharing that story, Tom went on to divulge that John had never hugged Tom even one time his entire life, nor had he ever told Tom he loved him. The same was true about his mother, Elinor; his grandmother Flossie; and grandfather Leland. Displays of love, affection, and affirmation were things that Tom just never knew.

Tom looks back and says, "That was my experience with parents. Thank God he never raised me. I'd never be the man I am today. He was a very selfish man."

Tom left his Emerson Electric job after only a few weeks to take a better one with Riviera Kitchens, a cabinet-manufacturing company. He was still without a car, but since the job wasn't that far away, he walked, hitching a ride as often as he could. One morning, he was walking down the Garden of the Gods Road on his way to work with his thumb up.

A guy in a beautiful brand-new red Mustang pulled up and offered him a ride. "Where ya headed?" asked the middle-aged man.

"To work, at Riviera Kitchens," Tom replied.

The man grinned and responded, "Me too! Hop in!"

His name was Phil, and he turned out to be the general foreman of the plant! What an amazing stroke of luck for that kid. Phil got to know Tom and took a strong liking to him, picking him up every morning to ride to work together until he could get his own car.

Tom's dad had a station wagon sitting in the driveway that was rarely ever used, so he decided one day to let Tom drive it to work, rather than making him walk or hitch a ride with Phil (Tom still had to walk to John's house to get the car, park it there when he got back, and walk home again). The Garden of the Gods Road was always busy, loaded up with tourists gawking at the interesting rock formations there. On the one day that Tom was allowed to use John's car, he ran into a major traffic jam. He had a can of soda with him that morning. When he hit his brakes for the traffic jam, the can tipped over and spilled soda all over the floorboard. Since he was on his way to work, and already slowed down by the traffic mess, he had no time to clean it up. Likewise, by the time he got back, it was late and dark, so he went on home expecting to take care of it in the morning.

Tom recalls John's reaction when he showed up the next morning, "Boy, did he lose his temper. My dad got really mad for bringing his car back looking like that. He told me I was never gonna drive it again, that I couldn't take care of anything. 'You've got a lot to learn, boy,' he said to me."

It was back to bumming a ride with Phil.

Tom had been working at Riviera Kitchens for a few weeks when his dad finally offered to help him out with his transportation issue. He cosigned on a car for Tom, a '58 Chevy for $250, $15 down and $25 a month payments. The old car required a bit of extra care, so it was fortunate that Tom met Bill, a guy at work who was pretty handy with cars.

Tom had worked his way up to head sander and was responsible for the entire Sanding Department. Bill was one of his crew. Tom and Bill were solid friends, but they sure didn't start out that way. When a Paint Room position opened up, Tom wanted to make the move. The problem was that Tom needed to backfill his position as head sander with a capable person.

Tom recalls, "I watched the guys work, and they just weren't very good at it. But Bill was. He was damn good at it, but he had an attitude. He had been dishonorably discharged from the military because he broke a cue stick over his sergeant's head!"

Bill's reputation as a hothead and a brawler preceded him, and he apparently wanted to pick a fight with this Tom kid. Bill provoked Tom on a regular basis by eating peanuts and leaving the shells lying all around the work floor. He tossed them onto Tom's worktable and even bounced them off Tom's head and shoulders from time to time. Every time Tom asked him to stop, he was met with all sorts of verbal abuses and threats from Bill.

One day, as this juvenile display was going on, Bill didn't realize he was being watched. Perched above the work floor was a bank of glass windows where Tom's friend Phil, the general foreman, was taking it all in.

He walked down to Tom, pulled him aside, and said, "I've been watching this guy, and I've had enough of it. I don't want to lose you, Coryell. You're doing good work. We're going to fire this man, just wanted you to know."

As Phil turned to leave, Tom realized that firing Bill would be bad if he ever hoped to get out of the Sanding Department and into the Paint Room.

"Wait a minute, Phil," replied Tom. "Bill's the only one I know who can sand these cabinets the way they're supposed to be. He's very good at it."

Phil responded, "I don't know, Tom, he's nothing but trouble."

Tom said, "Just talk to him first before you fire him."

Phil agreed and called Bill into the office. Down on the floor, Tom continued to work. He had a clear line of sight into the office to watch as Phil and Bill carried on the conversation. Phil did most of the talking, while every so often, Bill turned his head to look down at Tom, nodding slowly with a straight face. Tom felt an edge of anxiety begin to grow, hoping that he wasn't about to get a cue stick busted over his head—or worse!

They finished their meeting, and Bill came walking out onto the floor directly at Tom. *Oh boy, here we go.* Bill stopped in front of Tom and stuck his hand out. Surprised, Tom reached out and shook Bill's hand.

Bill spoke, "I'm really sorry for being such an asshole to you. Phil told me the reason I'm still here is because of you. You saved my job. I'll never forget that."

Tom moved up to Paint Room foreman, Bill took over as head sander, and the two became the best of friends.

On one particular Monday morning, Tom was getting clocked in to start his workweek when his buddy Bill came strolling in with a skip in his step, whistling a cheery little tune.

"What are you all happy about?" asked Tom with an amused smile.

"I met the girl I'm gonna marry!" replied Bill.

"Really! Do you know her?" asked Tom.

"Nope. I just met her Saturday. She was my waitress at a restaurant I stopped in at. Her name is Nancy. We looked at each other and knew immediately. She even asked me to marry me right there on the spot! But I just laughed it off."

Bill proceeded to tell Tom how the two met out in front of the restaurant after Nancy got off work. As she came out, Bill walked up to her all smiling, gave her a big hug, and they started to slow-dance together right there on the sidewalk. She asked him again to marry him, and he said YES! To this day, Tom just shakes his head in disbelief about that story.

He recalls with a big bright smile, "Crazy! So they got married, and that's how they met! Bill and Nancy, and me and Isabelle, we were like cousins. We were family. We did everything together!"

The two guys shared many good times together. Tom tells the story of a particularly memorable outing they once had where they drove the old Chevy way out into the countryside. They parked near a small lake to hunt rabbits.

As they were walking around to the other side of the lake, Bill said, "Hey look! There's a rabbit over by your car!"

Tom spotted the game and pulled back on his bow. The arrow flew, but was off the mark. It missed the rabbit, struck the gravel, bounced up, and flew right under the car, making a rather loud, metallic thump. *Uh-oh*, the two thought. They ran back over to the car and looked underneath to see a steady stream of gasoline squirting out of an arrow-sized puncture in the gas tank!

"Oh my god! We'd better go right now and find a gas station, or we'll be stuck out here," Tom exclaimed.

They did just that, fortunately finding a station a few miles away where a mechanic plugged the leak for them with a screw and rubber gasket.

"It's still in there as far as I know! It never leaked again!" says Tom, laughing out loud at the memory.

They played sports together as well, enjoying many hours of basketball, handball, and softball. Their softball team even won several league tournaments.

Tom says with a smile, "In fact, I still have my hat. It has a '#1 Riviera Kitchens' pin on it!"

They continued to enjoy their friendship and their jobs at Riviera Kitchens. Tom was a natural in the Paint Room. Even he didn't realize he had such a knack for it as he developed methods and procedures that not only enhanced the quality of the finished product, but doubled production by figuring out a way to reduce paint room time. It wasn't long before Tom was promoted to Paint Room foreman. Likewise, Bill's Sanding Department hummed like a well-oiled machine, moving product through like clockwork.

It came as no surprise that those two guys were top-of-mind with management when the company announced expansion plans for two new plants in Minnesota and Ohio. They had both built solid reputations for delivering top-quality results that produced real dollars for the company. Phil approached Tom one day to ask if he would be interested in moving to the brand-new, state-of-the-art Bel Air plant in Red Wing, Minnesota. He was immediately excited. Not only would it mean more opportunity for him to move up in the company, but he had always held a particular interest in the northern woodlands. But he wasn't sure.

Tom really loved his life in Colorado Springs and his friendship with Bill. "We were like brothers," says Tom.

But there was another motivating factor for him to want to leave Colorado Springs. It was John Daniel. The relationship he had hoped for with his father was going nowhere. The rifle situation was a very strong push away for Tom. In fact, after that happened, he found himself spending nearly all of his free time with Bill and almost none with John.

Riviera's senior management needed some extra convincing to approve Tom for the Minnesota move, simply because he was still just a kid.

Tom recalls, "They told me nobody had ever worked at that company as a foreman at my age before. They had a policy to be at least twenty-one, and even preferred you to be twenty-five. But Phil spoke up for me because of what me and Bill had done for the company."

With Phil as his advocate, Riviera management agreed to give Tom a shot and offered him a foreman position at the new Minnesota plant. Bill was offered a foreman position as well, at the new plant in Lancaster, Ohio.

Feeling accomplished, and a bit proud of that remarkable achievement, Tom decided to share the good news with his dad. Sadly, Tom did not receive the fatherly response he had hoped for. There were no "congratulations, son" remarks, and nothing remotely close to "I'm proud of you." In fact, it was quite the opposite.

Tom recalls his reaction, "He went off the deep end. He got real mad and started yelling. He told me I can't leave Colorado Springs, and he wanted me to be a plumber."

Tom had told John on more than one occasion that he didn't want to be a plumber. It simply wasn't something he wanted to do. But for whatever reason, John fully expected that Tom would follow in his footsteps. When Tom reminded John of this fact, he went completely off the tracks.

"Well you're *not* going to Minnesota in that car! I'm a cosigner for it, and I'll be over in the morning to pick it up!" screamed John.

His true colors were undeniable. All doubt was removed in that moment as Tom realized he was making the right choice to get away from that man. Perplexed, he called on the one guy he trusted most.

Tom: "What am I gonna to do, Bill?"

Bill: "You got the job in Minnesota for sure, right?"

Tom: "Yeah, but he's coming here in the morning to take my car away."

Bill: "No, he's not. You're not gonna be there. We're gonna go get a U-Haul right now."

Nancy and Isabelle started packing immediately. Bill and Tom went and got the U-Haul and recruited a few helpers from the softball team.

Tom recalls, "I never told my dad, and by midnight, we were gone."

They made it all the way to a rest stop near Burlington, Colorado, close to the Kansas border over 150 miles away. He was totally exhausted after working a full day, packing up his whole house, and driving since midnight. After only a four-hour nap in the car, Isabelle nudged him awake, and they were back at it. Tom drove straight through to Red Wing, Minnesota, over eight hundred miles away.

"I couldn't' do that again today!" Tom laughs.

Tom and Bill stayed in touch with each other over the years. Tom made trips to visit Bill. Bill made trips to visit Tom. Tom even moved back to Colorado Springs at one point after Bill had returned there in the 1980s. That didn't work out, but even to this day, the two are great friends. Bill is in Arizona, Tom is in Tennessee, and they're looking forward to their next golfing trip together.

Chapter Five

Steve's Story

Tom turned twenty in July of 1966 and had just been promoted into a foreman position at his job with Riviera Kitchens. He was doing such a good job for them that they offered to move him to their brand-new facility in Minnesota. This was unheard-of at the company. Promotions and management-level relocations were reserved for tenured, senior staff. This was a just a kid who was moving up the ladder quickly. Tom moved across four states, with his even younger wife, Isabelle (eighteen), and infant son, Danny (about one).

Tom recalls the first couple of weeks there, "We stayed with one of the plant managers, Bill—another Bill! He had eleven kids! Can you imagine? Talk about a 'Peyton Place'!

Those of a certain age will get that reference, but that was Bill's home. Tom and Isabelle shared a couch.

With only one bathroom in the house, Bill made sure to tell them, "Do yourself a favor and get up early before the girls do or you're not going to get in there!"

Tom recalls with a laugh, "I sure learned how to hold things!"

That only lasted a couple weeks until they found an apartment and settled in to their new home. Tom had seen some hard winters before in Pekin, Illinois, but he was about to be introduced to Minnesota.

TOM

He recalls a memory from his first winter there, "That was the heaviest snow and ice I had ever seen. The roads were so bad that when I stepped outside onto the driveway to go to work one morning, I slipped, fell down on a sheet of ice, and slid all the way down the hill, across the road, and into the ditch. I got up to start walking back up the hill, and here comes my lunch box sliding down the hill at me!"

While working there in Red Wing, Tom came to know one of the people on his crew, Dolores. She invited him to dinner, where Tom and Isabelle shared a pleasant evening with Dolores and her husband, Fred. Fred was about forty-two and shared Tom's interest in archery and hunting. With money being tight, and also being new to Minnesota, Tom divulged to Fred that he had no place to hunt or a very good bow to use. So Fred hooked him up, loaning him a quality hunting bow, and introduced him to a friend who had some property just over the border in Wisconsin.

That particular bow was quite unique and remains forever etched into Tom's memory. The old bow was a vintage three-piece unit, jointed in the middle, for easy breakdown and reassembly for convenient storage and transport.

"Very unusual, so you can imagine how old it is now," says Tom.

The young hunter ventured out in the Wisconsin backwoods to test his beginner's luck with deer hunting. He didn't have the luxury of a tree stand, so he proceeded to climb up a tree for a good vantage point, sitting on a limb.

"My butt could handle it in those days." Tom chuckles.

After some time had passed, he heard something approaching through the brush. He carefully pulled out an arrow for the ready, but noticed a big clump of mud on the broadhead from when he had stuck it in the ground to climb the tree. While looking in the direction of the noise coming his way, he attempted to blindly tap the arrow against the tree to knock off the dirt, but instead of hitting the tree, the sharp edge of that broadhead landed directly on the string of the bow, cutting it cleanly. As the tautness of the bow string let loose, the top limb went flying in one direction, knocked the arrow out of his hand, and the bottom limb flew the other direction, leaving Tom sitting there up a tree holding only a bow handle, a dangling string, with the arrow and the other two pieces of the bow laying on the ground below!

Tom says, "I never did see a deer, but I sure made a mess of that guy's bow!"

Fred decided to take Tom over to meet Bibbs and Orville, who were some extended family members. They also owned some property in Wisconsin. This is when Tom met Orville's son, Steve. Steve was also a young, bowhunting enthusiast learning the craft, so he and Tom hit it off quite well.

Tom finally found some success bowhunting on their farm, taking a raccoon as his first kill. Bibbs knew just what to do with the coon, cooking up a barbecue dinner and sharing a wonderful evening of hunting stories one evening. Tom and Steve made plans for their next hunting excursion.

By that time, Tom wanted to get his own hunting bow. He went to the local Erikson's Sporting Goods store that week and bought himself a nice Damon-Howatt 50-pound recurve.

"Which my son owns today," says Tom.

Tom and Steve spent many hours out in the woods hunting for deer and building a solid friendship all through that 1966 season.

As Tom puts it, "We hunted the entire season for deer, right up to December 31."

Having seen only one deer, and never having got a shot off, the young men were beginning to wonder if they would ever get the chance. Even if they did, Tom wondered if he would even be able to kill one if it were standing right in front of him. Steve was at least impressed with Tom's backyard practice shots into hay bales and paper plates.

"Steve wasn't even close," says Tom with a grin.

On that cold afternoon of December 31, 1966, snow covering the ground, and only a few hours of daylight remaining in the season, Steve began to wonder what they should do. Tom mentioned the name of someone he knew from his Riviera Kitchens job who had told him about seeing three deer all the time on their little three-acre farm surrounded by cornfields. Tom was told he was welcome to hunt there if he wanted to.

After hearing this, Steve said, "I know them! They live right down here!" motioning in the direction of their place. "Let's go try!"

So off they went, hoping for a change in luck and maybe even getting a shot at a fox. They selected a strategic spot near a fence line looking out over an open cornfield. They made plans for a drive.

For those unfamiliar with the practice, a *drive* is where one hunter takes a position near a tree line to watch for deer while another person hikes around that patch of woods to the other side and walks through it, intentionally making noise in order to move any deer that may be in there toward the waiting hunter. Because Steve knew very well that Tom was the better shot, he volunteered to hike up and around the woods to drive the deer toward Tom. Tom got nestled into his spot, sitting on the cold ground, leaning back against a fence post in his red-and-yellow Pekin, Illinois, High School letterman's coat.

"With my patches—*P*! That's how I hunted! I had no idea deer couldn't see color, but I sure stood out," says Tom with a giggle.

Several minutes passed when Tom noticed some movement, spotting three other hunters walking across the field about eighty yards away. They appeared to be young teenagers carrying a small .22 rifle, probably squirrel hunting.

"That's a big sport in Wisconsin, shooting squirrels," says Tom.

At just about the same time, those three deer that he and Steve had come for stepped out into the field. Tom's adrenaline immediately spiked, and he felt an instant surge of excitement only to realize that the deer were moving away from him toward the teenagers.

Oh no! he thought to himself.

About halfway into the field, the deer spotted the boys and got spooked. They turned tail and ran full speed right in Tom's direction.

"I mean, now they're coming lickety-split," says Tom.

With almost no time to react, Tom pulled back on his bow and let an arrow fly at the first deer running across his sights. To his surprise, he landed a perfect shot. Down went the deer, hard, sliding on the ground into a tree stump, and flipped head over heels into the air, lying motionless.

"I can still see it like a motion picture," recalls Tom.

The other two deer stopped in their tracks, not quite sure what to do with what they had just seen. Likewise, in a moment of astonishment, Tom sat there processing the scene, mesmerized by how his bow had just performed.

Wow! I didn't know it could to that! thought Tom.

He quickly reloaded his bow with another arrow from his quickie-quiver as one deer veered away toward the farmhouse. The other deer was still standing there, but when Tom moved the bow into position for a shot, the deer spotted the movement and darted toward the fence. Tom let loose the arrow and landed another great shot, only it was slightly off the mark, not delivering an immediate kill. Weakened by the arrow it had just taken, the deer attempted to jump the fence, hit the top wire with its chest, and flipped over backward onto the ground.

Again, Tom was stunned at what had just happened. The deer regained its footing, stood there for a moment, and snorted loudly at Tom. It regrouped, made another attempt to jump the fence, and cleared it. It rambled up a hill and lay down behind a V-shaped tree with only its head and ears visible.

"In Wisconsin, when I say *hill*, back where I'm from, that was a mountain," says Tom.

A few moments later, Steve came running up all excited from having seen the deer he was driving toward Tom.

"Did you see those deer! Which way did they go?" exclaimed Steve.

Tom proceeded to tell Steve about what had just happened, but Steve apparently thought Tom was telling a fib, because he cursed and yelled.

"C'mon! Where'd they go! We still got time to go get 'em!" urged Steve.

Just then, the three young boys that Tom had seen a few minutes before also came running up to the scene. They had seen the whole show.

TOM

"Steve! You won't believe what this guy did!"

Clearly these kids knew who Steve was and proceeded to gleefully tell him what they had just witnessed—two deer shot on a dead run!

Steve incredulously replied, "Really!"

Tom took Steve over to the deer lying dead on the ground.

"Oh my god, you did kill a deer!" said Steve.

Steve noticed the blood trail angling away from the kill toward the fence.

"Yeah, and that's from the other deer I shot," said Tom.

They walked over to the fence where Tom pointed out the V-shaped tree, holding Steve's head and pointing his eyes in the right direction.

"I see him! I see him! He's down!" said Steve.

Tom explained that the deer was gutshot, so they should wait a while.

"Let's have a cigarette and relax for a bit," suggested Tom.

After lighting a cigarette, Steve took one puff, threw the cigarette down.

"Okay! Let's go!" he hollered.

He proceeded to run up the hill toward the downed deer. Unable to stop the overexcited guy, Tom also ran up the hill behind Steve. With each step, they got more and more winded, getting closer to the deer. They were so exhausted that they were barely able to stand, going to one knee panting. Finally, they reached the deer. Steve insisted on making the final kill shot. Tom told him to get close, about five feet or so, and shoot the arrow into the neck for a swift, mercy kill. Steve pulled back, let loose the arrow, and missed! The deer jumped up, ran about twenty yards and lay back down again.

"Get up there and shoot him!" exclaimed Tom.

But Steve missed again! Tom decided to take a more strategic position for Steve's third try, circling around to the other side of the deer. But before Steve could take a third shot, the deer got up again, running straight at Tom, grunting, with antlers angled down in a full charge. Tom leaped aside, and the deer kept going. Tom swung around, raised his bow, and quickly loosed an arrow. He landed a perfect shot, directly into the back of the deer's head. The deer went down dead.

Steve stood there in disbelief at what he had just seen. "Did you really just do that!"

With a shoulder shrug, Tom said, "I guess I was just lucky."

A week later, Tom received a phone call from a friend. "Did you see the newspaper?" they asked.

Somehow, the story got out, and the local gazette ran a piece titled, "The Robin Hood of Ellsworth," reporting the first deer known to be taken by bow and arrow in the county.

"I made history! Me and Steve," Tom says with a chuckle.

That experience formed the basis of a solid and lasting friendship between the two young men, sharing a love of the outdoors, archery, and hunting.

For the next couple of years, 1966–1968, Tom continued hunting with his best friend Steve, and earning a modest living with Riviera Kitchens. Tom's church life had grown significantly during this time, serving as youth pastor and Boys' Brigade leader. He played piano and gained the love and respect of his pastor and the church family. That was an area of Tom's life that Steve did not have in common. Despite Tom's many attempts to coax Steve into it, the man simply did not have an interest in God or the church.

Tom's life was about to change around that time. He began to realize that he needed to make more money. A second child was on the way, and his meager union wages of $2.35 an hour would simply not cut it. Isabelle's dad just so happened to be fairly high up in the Caterpillar Company as a safety officer back in Illinois, near his hometown of Pekin, and offered to help Tom get hired on.

Tom needed to make a trip to Illinois in order to submit his job application to Caterpillar and complete an aptitude test. So in the fall of 1967, he and his pregnant wife, Isabelle, decided to make a family visit out of it. Tom had managed to upgrade his vehicle by that time, trading in the old '58 Chevy for a much nicer '62 Ford Falcon. They loaded up the car with little Danny in the front seat between them and made the drive to Pekin to stay with Thomas and Bobbye for a few days while Tom worked on his Caterpillar paperwork.

TOM

Tom says, "On the way there, we had a horrible accident."

On a rural stretch of wet, rainy Illinois highway, Tom went to pass a slower car and went into a skid. The car spun out of control, around and around, sliding off the road and into a culvert. It flipped upside down, landing squarely on the roof, and continued to slide down the middle of the road, wheels up, and slid off the road again into the ditch, narrowly missing a telephone pole.

Tom recalls, "When I knew we were gonna flip over, I just lay over the seat and grabbed everybody and held them down. We didn't have seat belts in those days, so I grabbed the bottom of the seat, lay across them, and became a human seat belt."

There was this young family, standing in the rain next to an upside-down, smashed-up car, after having crawled through a busted rear window—a pregnant woman and a man holding a little boy. Amazingly, no one was injured.

"It was pouring down rain. Not one car opened their windows and offered us help! Nobody! I couldn't believe it. That's Illinois though. People are weird there," says Tom.

Apparently, the car he tried to pass didn't stop either and left them there in the rain. They walked into a nearby yard along the roadside, and a woman came out of the house to place a coat on Isabelle and invited them inside. The wreck had been called in by that time, so Tom went back to the scene to work out the cleanup details with the authorities. Running on adrenaline through the ordeal, Tom felt no pain or injuries and got through it all.

"Except for the next day, I could hardly move. I had bruises all over me," recalls Tom.

Tom's father-in-law came and got them from the crash scene. Isabelle's parents were a huge help during this time, getting Tom back and forth to Caterpillar to finish his paperwork, then returning the family to Red Wing. When he got back, Tom's neighbor helped him find an old 1958 Ford for $50.

"And if you saw the car, it was probably worth less!" says Tom, laughing at the memory.

With wobbly headlights, holes in the floorboard, Tom was reduced to driving that old jalopy for several years while paying for the once-beautiful, now-wrecked Falcon.

But as fortune would have it, "It ran! You couldn't hurt this car!" says Tom.

All through that harsh 1967 Minnesota winter, the old Ford started every day for Tom, getting him back and forth to work. During that winter, January 16, 1968, is when Tom's second son was born—Steven Scott, in honor of his two closest hunting friends.

"We had a horrible blizzard the night before. The snow was so bad," recalls Tom.

Isabelle went into labor that evening, and Tom had to get the old car warmed up and ready to go. Slipping and sliding all the way through the deep snow, the old Ford got them to the doctor's office. While standing there at the check-in counter, her water broke.

Tom recalls, "The nurse went off the deep end. "Oh my god! Get her out of here! She's having her baby! Get her to the hospital now!"

With their help, Tom managed to get Isabelle back out to the car. Fortunately, the hospital was only about four or five blocks down the road. Once again, swishing and sloshing through the deep snow, Tom arrived at the hospital. They were waiting for Isabelle with a wheelchair and rushed her in right away. Tom had to take little Danny to the babysitter, so off he went again into the snow-covered streets of Red Wing, all the way back home to the neighbors, and all the way back to the hospital again.

As he walked back into the hospital, he caught the eyes of a nurse carrying a baby across the hallway who promptly announced, "It's a boy!"

With palms up and jaw dropped, "What!" exclaimed Tom.

Expecting hours of labor, he was completely surprised that little Steve was already there.

"Steve never did like to wait very long. When he wanted to do something, he went for it!" Tom laughs.

A few months went by, and he finally got the call from Caterpillar. He got the job!

TOM

"I'd start out at $3.50 an hour. A whole lot more than what I was making!" says Tom.

All he had to do was show up on July 8, 1968, to start his new job. Tom started packing right away and began making his farewells. His pastor urged him not to go, believing that God had called Tom to his current place. The youth program was flourishing, but Tom was driven by the practical need to earn more money to support his family. He declined to stay. Relenting to Tom's decision, the pastor invited him to play piano at the next Sunday service for his final visit and to share his testimony.

Tom made a phone call to his buddy Steve, telling him the news, and asked him if he would come to church for his last Sunday there. Steve refused, even after Tom pleaded, saying it might be the last time they would ever see each other. Tom even made the drive out to Steve's Wisconsin home to beg him one last time in person.

"I'm just not ready, Tom," said Steve.

His final Sunday arrived. Tom was sitting at the piano on the church stage preparing to lead the congregation in song and to take the pulpit to offer his testimony when he spotted a familiar head of hair way in the back row trying hard to not be noticed. It was Steve.

The service commenced, Tom did his part, and the pastor delivered a great salvation message. The service went into its final moments, with Tom playing soft piano music while the pastor made the invitation—over and over, but Steve did not budge! Tom had warned the pastor this might happen, but he tried and tried, to the point where Tom began to feel embarrassed. Steve never did come forward.

The service ended, and folks filtered outside, saying their goodbyes to the young family—Tom, Isabelle, Danny, and baby Steve. Standing off to the side, Steve waited his turn to hug his buddy goodbye and to wish him well. Their final exchange went something like this:

> Tom: "You know we'll never see each other again."
> Steve: "Yes, we will! Even if I have to come to Illinois to hunt, we'll get together again."

Tom: Stony silence.

Steve: "I know what you were doing in there. I know what you want. I'm just not ready."

Tom: "When will you know you're ready?"

Steve: "I don't know! I'll just know, okay!"

In that moment, Tom felt a strange movement in his spirit, an anguish of the soul. Tom grabbed Steve by his shirt collar, pulled his face close, and cried out in loud desperation, "Steve! In the last fleeting seconds of your life, call upon Jesus! He will save you!"

In shocked bewilderment, Steve tried to pull away from Tom, but he pulled him close again, repeating the plea with even more gusto. "Steve! In the last fleeting seconds of your life, call upon Jesus! He *will* save you!"

People heard the commotion and began to gather around the two men, wondering if a fight was about to erupt. But the feeling left Tom just as quickly as it had come.

Steve pulled away, saying, "Okay, okay!"

The pastor asked if things were okay. Tom said, "Yes, it's fine," apologized, and all went calm again.

In a strange moment of acknowledgement, Steve's eyes locked with Tom's as if to say, "I understand," and the two simply walked away.

Feeling weird, and in disbelief over the way he had just behaved, Tom got into his car with his family.

Isabelle asked, "What was that all about?"

Tom replied, "I have no idea."

He gazed back up the hill where Steve was still standing, watching Tom leave. With the sun shining brightly at his back, a silhouette of the cross over his shoulder, and the church building perched behind him, an indelible picture was forever etched upon Tom's memory as that was the last moment he ever saw his friend Steve.

Chapter Six

Odie and Dale

Finally, July 8, 1968, arrived. It was Tom's first day on the new Caterpillar job. After checking in with the HR department and completing more paperwork, he was told he would start out in the foundry as a mold floor cleaner.

Tom recalls with a grin, "That was a fancy word for using a broom."

After completing the lengthy orientation process, Tom and four other new hires showed up at the foundry for their first shift the next day. Of course, it was the night shift for the five new guys. Among the group was a man named Odie, assigned as the lead guy for the team. Tom, Odie, and the team were promptly met by the foundry foreman, Mr. Blackard.

With a grin, Tom remembers the guy distinctly, "He was about as black as he could be for an African American. But that was his name, Mr. Blackard."

He was a giant of a man too, as Tom recalls. Not fat, but built like the kind of guy you don't want to mess with. With a gleam in his eye, Mr. Blackard informed the new crew that the office people had lied to them.

"I don't even know what a mold floor cleaner is. Around here, if we don't get it with a shovel, we don't mess with it," said the foreman.

He handed Tom a shovel, asked him how it felt, and Tom responded, "Fine."

With an ornery grin, Mr. Blackard proclaimed, "Never made a mistake yet! I can fit anybody with a shovel!"

The crew was taken to where they would be working. Stretched out before them were metal stairs leading down into a long pit, about thirty yards in length, where the steps disappeared into the dirt. Over time, sand, filings, and various materials had built up from all the mold work going on above it.

Mr. Blackard said, "There's a floor about four feet down. We want to get down to that."

That was the job. Over the next six backbreaking months, eight hours a day, the five guys cleaned that floor. In some places of the corridor, it narrowed, turned, and shortened to the point where they were working on their knees. After that dirty job, Tom was moved up to the mold floor level as a flask cleaner.

Still dirty work, Tom recalls how hot it was, "They were called ovens, and, boy, was it ever."

So hot, in fact, that they allowed him to enter for only ten minutes at a time. After paying his dues on that job for a while, he was moved up again to the line, assisting with the iron pouring process. Tom recalls how the giant buckets of molten metal would swing over his head into position for the pour. Being within five to ten feet of the pour, it would sometimes pop and pelt everyone with hot iron.

"We were so hot and sweaty, it bounced right off. You don't ever want to work there if you don't sweat. Sometimes it leaves a little mark," says Tom.

On one occasion, one of Tom's coworkers came running up to him, turned him around, and grabbed a hand towel that was in his back pocket that Tom had been using to wipe the sweat from his face. The thing had caught fire, and Tom was burning!

It was during that time, working hard on the Caterpillar foundry job that Tom developed a working relationship with the team leader, Odie. Tom describes Odie as a vulgar man. Just about everything that came out of his mouth was cursing and swearing.

"I think he even embarrassed the devil," recalls Tom with a chuckle.

It was also during this time that Tom got involved with the First Baptist Church in Pekin. In fact, it was the same church Tom had gone to as a boy. On one particular Sunday, Pastor Don delivered a stirring sermon that moved something in Tom. The message was about sharing your faith. Being a Christian is not enough, you need to be an example and witness to those around you.

"People right next to us are dying and going to hell, and you didn't even tell them about the Savior?" Tom recalls the message.

A particular person came into Tom's mind when he heard those words—Odie. Not one to back away from his convictions, Tom began to witness to the most vulgar man he had ever met. Of course, he was met right away with anger and cursing when Tom tried to tell Odie about Jesus. Tom invited him to church anyway. On and on Odie went, foul mouth and all. On and on Tom went, sharing his faith as often as he could, even offering to pick him up and drive him to church. One day, Odie finally relented and agreed to go!

Sunday came. Tom got up early to make the drive into Peoria to pick up Odie and his wife. When she answered the door, it was obvious that she was not expecting him. When Tom explained why he was there, the woman informed him that Odie would not be going to church. He was drunk and passed out cold. He would probably not wake up until it was time to go to back to work. Back on the job, Odie angrily told Tom to leave him alone and to stop preaching to him.

"My mother is always praying for me and crying, and I just don't want to hear it anymore!" Odie complained.

Tom let it go and never bothered Odie again on the matter, but Odie's story doesn't end there. It will conclude with "Danny's Story."

Dale was another guy that Tom had met on the job at Caterpillar. Having worked his way up the ladder a bit, Tom was promoted to an inspector position. He had a thirteen-person line crew, and Dale was one of the thirteen.

"Dale was a wild guy, but he liked to hunt," says Tom.

That was the common thread, once again, that connected Tom to another friend. A shared love for the outdoors and hunting. Dale's father had a six hundred-acre place near Forest City, loaded with pheasants, so Tom and Dale became pretty good friends.

"We shot pheasants like you wouldn't believe! My gun got so hot I had to take a break!" says Tom.

Like he did with Odie, Tom felt a tug on his heart to witness and share Christ with his hunting buddy. Dale was very different. He was actually interested. He listened intently and asked a lot of questions. Tom asked if he could come to his house some time to talk more with him and his wife. Dale said yes.

On the very next Sunday, Tom received another stirring message at church. It was about how to share the Gospel the right way, and he learned an effective method for making the invitation. Tom was alone that particular Sunday because Isabelle and the boys were homesick. While driving home, the Lord placed Dale strongly upon Tom's heart. So intense was the feeling, that he turned the car around right at that moment and drove straight to Dale's house.

As fate would have it, both Dale and his wife were home. They welcomed Tom in. As he began to share, Tom found himself using some of the very same techniques he had just learned about a couple hours before. To his amazement, both Dale and his wife got up from the couch and knelt beside Tom to pray the sinner's prayer that very afternoon. Both accepted Christ! What a blessing!

Dale's family had experienced some significant loss in their lives. Both of Dale's older brothers had died in tragic events some years before. The oldest brother was killed in a terrible car accident on the road right in front of the family home. The middle bother suffered a severe head injury in an accidental discharge of a pellet gun while boarding the bus for school, again, right in front of the house. That injury had put the boy in a wheelchair, and in time, complications from the injury took his life.

Dale's parents had buried two sons. He was the only one left. Could it be that this was enough sorrow and loss for one family? Sadly, no. Because barely two weeks to the day that Dale and his wife knelt with Tom to accept Christ, Dale suffered the same horrible fate that his big bother did so many years before. While driving to his mom and dad's house, he lost control of the vehicle, spun out, and rolled over. In a strange and tragic twist of fate, the accident occurred right in front of the family home, again. The car rolled over in such a way that it had come to rest just a few steps away from the front porch.

Tom describes the scene, shaking his head, visibly moved by the telling of the story nearly fifty years later, "Dale was the only son that was left. And there . . . his mother came out . . . and right there again, at the same farm home, same road . . . she had no more children left. Nobody to be an heir to . . . not a daughter, nobody. They were all gone . . . man."

A couple of days later, as Tom was thinking about his friend Dale one evening, he felt a peculiar tug on his soul.

Tom recalls, "It really bothered me. I had to go out and talk to Dale's parents."

Compelled by this feeling, Tom drove all the way out to Forest City. The sun had set by that time, and it was dark as he knocked on the back door. Dale's father answered. Knowing Tom well from their pheasant hunting experiences together, he invited Tom inside. There in the center of the living room, with furniture pushed back against the walls, was a circle of people in fold-out chairs. Family, friends, folks whom Tom had never met before, all turned to see who was joining them in their somber gathering of grief.

In that moment of uncertainty, Tom realized the awkwardness of it, asking himself, *What do you tell a family, a mom and dad who've lost everything they ever loved? Their children are gone. Faith and hope are shattered. What do you say to a hopeless, broken soul in a situation like that?*

Tom recalls the moment, "But God went with me, and for some reason, he moved me to step right out into the middle of that room."

Filled with compassion, and with the Spirit, Tom proceeded to speak the words given to him in that crucible moment. It went something like this:

Tom: "You don't know me, but Dale's dad knows me." (He locked eyes with Dale's wife at that moment.) "And you know me, don't you?"

Dale's wife: "Yes."

Tom: "I want to tell you something about Dale you may not know. I went to Dale's house about two weeks ago." (He looked again at Dale's widow.) "You remember that, don't you?"

Dale's wife: "Yes, I do."

Tom: "I shared Jesus Christ with Dale that day." (The look on the faces of Dale's parents began to change.) "I asked him to receive Christ, and do you know that Dale and his wife both kneeled with me at the coffee table, and they asked Jesus into their lives and to forgive their sin? I was there. That really happened. Standing here, I now know why God wanted me to do that with your son. That's what I want you to know, and that it isn't hopeless. You will see him again one day."

The circle of people sat there in a moment of stunned silence, some crying, as Tom slowly exited the room. Dale's dad walked with Tom to the back door. He grabbed Tom and pulled him in tightly. Tom could feel warm tears running down the back of his neck as they embraced for a long moment.

Then he said, "Thank you for coming and sharing that story with me. You have no idea what that's done for me."

Tom never knew what became of that family. After Dale died, he didn't keep in touch. Tom holds on to the hope that by his example that day, those who witnessed something so special also decided to follow Jesus and were saved.

Chapter Seven

Danny's Story

IN ORDER TO finish Odie's story, the most painful experience of Tom's life must now be shared. Daniel Dean, Tom's firstborn son, was a big-eyed happy boy of four years in 1969. It was August. Fall was just a few weeks away, which meant hunting season was close. Tom had been moved off the third shift by this time and got off work at 3:00 p.m. This gave him a good chunk of time to work with his black Labrador, T-bone, training him to point, flush, retrieve, and all the great things those amazing hunting dogs can do. T-bone was an exceptional hound, but he had not yet mastered the skills for a duck hunt. Tom and his buddy Scott had been planning for months to get out into the field for ducks, so on one particular evening after arriving home from work, Tom began loading up the car for an evening with Scott to train T-bone how to retrieve ducks from the Little Mackinaw River.

His wife, Isabelle, stepped out and said, "Why don't you take Danny with you?"

The little guy was standing not far off by the fence talking with a neighbor kid and heard his mother's suggestion. Tom slowly turned his head in Danny's direction. Sure enough, he was staring right at his dad with a bright-eyed look. "Oh please, please!"

In his heart, Tom really wanted to take his son, but he knew that T-bone wouldn't work at all if Danny was there. T-bone loved that boy, and he would only want to play, so Tom decided to not take Danny.

After arriving at their spot on the river, Tom waited and waited for Scott to show up. Scott had the whistle, and Tom needed him there for the training, but apparently, Scott had forgotten and never showed up. Tom loaded up and headed back home. Before going home, he stopped by his brother Til's house. Tom's neighbor had been making complaints about leaving the dog tied up, so he decided to leave T-bone with his brother for a while. When Tom turned the corner onto his street, he saw a crowd of people, policemen, and squad cars all around. He pulled up quietly, wondering what in the world was going on.

His neighbor came running up and exclaimed, "Oh my god, Tom! Get to the hospital now! Your son's been hit by a car!"

In an instant wash of emotions, Tom dropped the car into reverse, swung it around, and peeled out, leaving black rubber on the road racing off to the hospital. He rushed into the emergency room to see his son's blood all over the floor and the curtain. A high school friend of Tom's from the football team, Bearde, was there.

Grabbing him, Bearde pleaded, "Tom, don't go in there. You don't want to see this!"

"I want to see him!" yelled Tom.

Others joined Bearde in restraining Tom, trying to prevent him from looking at the horrific scene. The injuries were far too severe for that small Pekin hospital to handle, and plans were already in motion to transfer Danny to Peoria Methodist.

"We can't help him here!" exclaimed an ER doctor.

In a sea of emotional turmoil, Tom was too upset to drive. He called his sister Carol to come and drive him over to the Peoria hospital. In heavy traffic, not quite sure where they were going, and caught up in the overwhelming emotion of the situation, Tom spotted a police car's running radar and told Carol to pull over. Tom ran up to the officer and explained what was happening and asked for an escort to the hospital.

"You follow me!" exclaimed the trooper, and off they went, lights and siren, right up to the front door of the hospital.

TOM

The hospital staff took Tom and Carol to a family waiting room while they worked on Danny. A deacon from the church arrived, consoling and praying with Tom. After getting Danny cleaned up and stabilized, they finally allowed Tom to see him.

With a broken, anguished voice, Tom recalls the memory, "What I was about to see would hurt any father."

Little Danny lay there, unconscious. The side of his head was caved in. A tongue compressor was in his mouth.

"He was lifeless," Tom whispers softly as he remembers the moment.

Isabelle got caught up in the rush after the accident, making arrangements for little Steve and such. It took some time before she finally arrived at the hospital. Tom's pastor had also arrived by that time, having canceled his vacation to be there for Tom and Isabelle. She went in to see her little boy, while Tom stayed out and prayed with Don.

Isabelle came out of Danny's room after a while, tears streaming down her face. "I sang his favorite song."

Through the tears, Isabelle looked at Tom and said, "Tom, he moved. He moved and tried to talk to me."

With great emotion, Tom recalls, "The song was 'He is able. He is able. I know my Lord is able to see me through.'"

Little Danny used to stand up tall on the pew at church, singing that song with all the fervor a four-year old can muster. Tom describes a young boy so in love with Jesus and the church that just two Sundays before the accident, this little boy heard the invitation from Pastor Don and tugged on his father's shirt sleeve.

"Daddy, I want to go down there."

Not quite sure what to do in that moment, Tom told him to wait until after church to talk about it and went back to singing the invitation hymn. Without hesitation, Danny leaped off the pew and marched right down to the pastor before Tom could even react to stop him. There, in front of God and everyone, Danny answered the call. He was the only one who went forward that day. As little Danny stood there looking up at the pastor, pulling on his pant leg, Don tried to ignore what was happening as he closed the invitation.

At the very moment, the music stopped, and the place went quiet; he looked down at Danny and exclaimed, "What!"

In an awkward moment, as annoyed churchgoers looked on with disapproval at this man's outburst, the pastor collected his composure and asked Danny, "What do you want, son?"

With the excited face that only a four-year-old child can produce, Danny proclaimed, "I want to ask Jesus into my heart! I want him to be *my* friend!"

Pastor Don motioned for the Sunday school teacher to take Danny to the front pew and talk to him. Tom watched the two as a few moments went by. Danny intently removed her hand from his, stepped forward resolutely, and proceeded to kneel at the bench with no adult assistance whatsoever, and prayed the sinner's prayer. In near disbelief at what he was witnessing, the pastor watched it all unfold, looking back at the congregation in astonishment.

Two weeks later, little Danny laid in the ICU with a crushed skull. Tom and Isabelle waited, prayed, and cried. Hardly eating or sleeping for two days, they went in and out of the room checking on their boy, hoping.

Tom anguished over not taking Danny to the river with him and T-bone. "I'm sorry for not taking you with me. I'm sorry," cried Tom softly.

During that time, a bothersome noise had started to fill the halls of the ICU. Way down at the end of the hall was the sound of a man moaning loudly, sometimes yelling. After some time of this going on, Tom's curiosity got the better of him. He went down there to check out the commotion. He stepped into the room and slowly pulled back the curtain to see a man lying there. He was not able tell who it was with all the bandages and tubes, but when the man saw Tom standing there, he went into a fit, kicking and screaming as if in great fear of something.

"No! No! Please no," the man cried out in terror.

An ICU nurse rushed in. "What did you do to him!" she demanded.

Tom responded, "Nothing. I just walked in to see what was going on."

TOM

"You need to leave," she said.

He went back to the waiting room. To his surprise, there sat Odie's wife. That screaming man was Odie. She explained to Tom that Odie was drunk at a bar a couple nights before when a fight broke out. In the chaos of the fight, someone smashed a barstool over his head, knocking him out cold. When he came to, he went on home and went to bed. She was unable to wake him up the next morning. Odie had been in the hospital ever since, coming in and out of consciousness, with a severe concussion. Odie did not survive the injury, passing away right there in that hospital bed.

While continuing to wait and hope, the doctor informed Tom and Isabelle that there was nothing more they could do. It was highly unlikely he would be waking up. Prayer was all that was left, so pray they did.

On one occasion, after Tom went in to check on Danny, he came out of the room to see a woman sitting in the hallway deeply upset. Even in the midst of his own personal tragedy, Tom took a moment to speak with the woman.

"What happened?" he asked.

"My daughter was hit by a car. They think she's going to die." She cried.

With his own son dying of the very same thing, Tom held that woman by the hand and prayed for the life of her child.

Near the end of his forty-eight-hour nightmare, short on sleep and food, Tom sat in a waiting room chair late into the night. Drifting off slightly, half asleep, Tom felt the physical touch of a hand on his cheek. Jerking awake with alarm, he stood up in a dimly lit, empty room. He looked all around, stepped out into the hallway, but no one was around. Tom walked back into the room and checked the clock. It was 6:00 a.m.

At that moment, a commotion erupted in Danny's room. Tom rushed in as the nurse called out for help, hollering emergency codes.

"We're losing him!"

With a sinking feeling in his soul, Tom experienced a strange sensation, as if time itself had slowed to a crawl. In those brief moments, as the ICU staff rushed to react to Danny's plummeting vital signs, little Danny opened his one, unbandaged eye and looked directly at Tom. He lifted his hand as if to say something, but was not able to speak with the compressor in his mouth.

In shock, Tom asked, "Are you okay?"

Danny slowly nodded his head yes.

"You're gonna be all right!" exclaimed Tom.

But Danny strongly shook his head no that time.

Tom leaned forward, reaching out to Danny, saying, "Yes, you are!"

Danny grabbed Tom by the finger, flashed him a gentle smile, softly tucked his daddy's finger up under his chin, and died.

In Tom's owns words, "It was so hard. I'll never get over it. I want to tell you this story because I want you to know that a little boy heard the Gospel, and he went and prayed to receive Christ when a full-grown man, who had wisdom and knowledge that God loved him, and his mom prayed for him, rejected Christ and went into a lost eternity. That's why he was screaming no. And the girl that survived . . . why? Do you think God's unjust? No. We don't know why all these things happened, but they did. That little girl lived, and that mother was so happy, and my son died. This story has been told over and over again over the years and has helped lead a lot of people to Christ. And I want you to know that it didn't change the way I felt about God one bit, because I know He is my only hope in this life."

On the very next Sunday after Danny's funeral, Tom, Isabelle, and little Steve sat there in the church congregation as Pastor Don began to deliver his sermon. He had planned to say some things about Danny's accident, but when he noticed Tom sitting in the audience, he immediately paused. He didn't expect to see Tom there so soon after such a terrible tragedy. Don's spirit stirred, anguished, tears swelled in his eyes.

In a broken voice, he locked eyes with Tom and spoke, "I am so sorry."

Turning his attention back to the crowd, he proclaimed, "Never again will I *ever* deny a child who comes to me and wants to know Christ!"

TOM

The sermon delivered that day was as authentic and genuine as it can get, dealing with the loss of a child and the impact of little Danny's salvation story just a week before his death. It wasn't long after those events that the children's ministry at that church exploded with tremendous growth. Many more kids were saved because of Danny.

Chapter Eight

More on Danny

Prior to that terrible day, things were going quite well for Tom and his young family. His job at Caterpillar had progressed to the point where he was working as an inspector, making a great wage. He had a happy home life with a wife and two boys, he had good friends to go hunting with, church was going great, and his relationships with local family in the Pekin/Peoria area were going well.

Just a few days before Danny's accident, something very strange happened to Tom. He was abruptly awakened in the middle of the night to the sound of his own screams. It was 4:00 a.m. Tom sat there in his bed shivering, crying, and covered in sweat. Isabelle was also awakened. She shook him, asking what happened. Tom was so shaken from the nightmare he had just witnessed in his dreams that he could not even speak. He had to be at work by 6:00 a.m. anyway, so the couple decided to go ahead and get up. As Isabelle started a pot of coffee, Tom sat at the kitchen table trying to calm himself down.

He finally collected his thoughts and told Isabelle, "I had a horrible, horrible nightmare. I dreamed that Danny ran out into the street and a white car hit him. It hit him right in the head, and I saw him flying way down the road. I ran out there and saw blood gushing out of his eyes and ears, and there was a guy there crying, 'I didn't see him!' while clawing and scraping the ground."

TOM

With a breaking, sobbing voice, Tom gasped through his tears, "I was there, Isabelle! It was so real! I saw it!"

After taking a moment to console her husband and calm him down, she took Tom by the hand and led him to Danny's bedroom. She slowly pulled back the blanket for Tom to see his precious little boy sleeping peacefully in his bed.

"It was just a nightmare, Tom, just a nightmare," she whispered.

It took some time that morning, but Tom was eventually able to shake the terrors from his mind and go about his day.

Tom recalls the memory, saying, "So I passed it off. But I'll tell you what, somebody told me what was coming. But I didn't understand it, and our church didn't believe in that kind of stuff, so I didn't worry."

As more details about the accident became known, Tom learned it was indeed a white car that struck Danny, driven by a young man who, according to witnesses, quite literally crawled around on the ground in grief and shock crying, "I didn't see him! I didn't see him!."

Witnesses also explained that a group of neighborhood kids were across the street in an open field area playing with a new toy, a water-propelled rocket. When Danny saw what they were up to, of course he wanted to get a closer look. What little boy in the 1960s didn't love rockets? The little four-year-old darted out into the street from in between a couple of parked cars and—

Was God attempting to prepare Tom for that event by giving him a glimpse of the horror ahead of time? Perhaps it was a way to acclimate Tom's soul for the horrible pain he was about to enter into? Was it a warning of some kind? God only knows. It is one of those questions that has driven Tom to share Danny's story and this book. The full-circle moment is still in question for Tom. The death of a child rarely ever makes sense to a grieving parent, even fifty years after the fact.

CHAPTER NINE

Life AD (After Danny)

IT PROBABLY COMES as no surprise that Tom's life was never the same after he buried his son. After the funeral, Tom locked himself away inside his home, alone in a dark bedroom, and refused to speak to the visitors who came to check on him. He cried and cried, cried himself into a splitting headache, then he cried some more. It was a grief beyond measure, a pain that only those who have been there can fully understand.

Tom recalls, "This went on for days. I had to stop crying, but there was nothing that could change it."

His pastor finally convinced Tom to get some counseling. Over time, the tears dried and were replaced with a hollow emptiness. Tom began to move forward, and life slowly took on the form of a "new normal."

Tom never returned to his job at Caterpillar. The family survived the next few years on insurance money, odd jobs, and help from family and the church. Somehow, in the midst of grief and despair, Tom and his wife, Isabelle, managed to bring two more children into the family. Rebecca Jane came along about a year after the funeral, interestingly on their wedding anniversary, September 26, 1970. Then David James arrived on May 5, 1972, strangely close to Danny's birthday.

TOM

Tom struggled to redefine his life. It was at about that time that the church proposed a life change to Tom. They offered to move him to Kansas City to attend the Calvary Bible College. Tom agreed.

Prior to leaving Pekin, Tom received word that his dad, John Daniel, had suffered a heart attack. John had moved back to Illinois to take a pipe-fitter job with the growing Caterpillar company, which had just opened a brand-new facility in the Pekin area. Despite the rocky relationship, the two had managed to visit each other a time or two since his return, so Tom decided to go see his dad at the hospital.

The visit was awkward, filled with small talk and silent moments. Tom told him about his plans to move away and start a new life in Kansas City. To Tom's surprise, John was clearly still fixated on the hope of Tom following in his footsteps to become a plumber. John offered to give him his 32 Degree Mason Ring as a token pledge if he would just stay and become a mason. But Tom's mind was made up. He told John that God had plans for him to start a new life.

Tom describes John's reaction, "His face hardened with a very ugly and angry look. He threw his fist in the air, right in my face, so I could see the ring up close, and he hollered, 'That's God!' I got up and left, feeling very sad. I never saw him again after that day."

With a chuckle, Tom says, "I learned some years later that the 'other' Ellinor gave my 30–06 and the ring to her son after dad died. Oh well."

Fred was a friend from the church who joined Tom in taking an initial trip to Kansas City to help him find a home near the college. Tom knew he needed to be close to school and that an apartment would not work for a family of five, so he and Fred drove around in circles for hours one day looking for a solution. They were hitting a dead end, so they decided to take a break. As luck would have it, there was a Brown's Chicken restaurant right on the corner near the college, so the two sat there and enjoyed a chicken dinner together.

Realizing that they were in need of some help to find the right place, they agreed it was time to pray. With sincere hearts, they asked for God to show them a place to live. The men left the restaurant and climbed back into the car to resume the search. They decided to head down a particular road they had not yet tried. It ran right alongside the college. When they came to a stop sign, Tom looked to his left and noticed a U-Haul truck sitting on the roadside right in front of a quaint little home. At that moment, two men emerged from the house carrying some furniture.

Tom said, "Do you see that, Fred?"

Sensing an immediate answer to prayer, Fred and Tom pulled the car up near the truck. They got out and introduced themselves to the other men. Both men were students at the college. One of them had just graduated and was moving out, and it was a rental house! The man gave them his landlord's contact information, and it all fell into place like clockwork.

The house was ideally sized for a big family; it had accommodations for Tom's mother and grandmother, who would be moving with them, and it was right across the street from the college. It was a perfect answer to their prayer. Praise Jesus!

The family packed up and made the long drive from Pekin, Illinois, to Kansas City, Missouri. Tom drove the U-Haul with little Steve in the passenger seat, while his wife, Isabelle, followed behind in the family car loaded with Tom's school supplies, little Becky and David, Tom's mother, Elinor, and grandmother Flossie. After a full day of driving, the family continued working into the night getting the truck unloaded and beds set up for everyone. Exhausted, tired, and worn-out from the long day, Tom finally reached a stopping point and called it a night. He had forgotten to unload the car with all his school supplies inside, including a typewriter, a calculator, and various other supplies.

Tom recalls, "I woke up the next morning, and the back doors of the car were open, and somebody had stolen everything. I had *nothing*—no typewriter, not a thing!"

With a chuckle, Tom says, "That was my beginning of school. Satan sure tried to discourage me."

As with most colleges, Calvary requires an entrance exam to assess where a student's strengths are. Tom's test results were not that great, so the school placed him on probation. One counselor had even advised him against going at all because the scores indicated he would be a D student at best. They underestimated Tom's determination. Contrary to the counselor's guidance against it, despite his low test scores, and regardless of his academic weakness, Tom forged ahead to make three Bs and two Cs in his first semester. The college promptly removed Tom from probation.

Thoughts of little Danny still darkened Tom's soul from time to time, but he kept his mind occupied as a working student. He worked hard, studied hard, and learned a ton of great theology. He continued to do well in all his courses over the next two years.

It was during this time that Tom met an interesting fellow named Hoyt. Hoyt was a maintenance worker at the college, who had developed a friendship with Tom. In a casual conversation one day, Tom divulged to Hoyt that he had some money he was thinking about investing. It was some leftover life insurance money from Danny's death. Hoyt told Tom about some property called Carolika Lakes that he'd had his eyes on for years. He dreamed of turning it into a Bible camp, but didn't have the money to make it happen. Tom agreed to go out to the property with Hoyt to have a look and to meet the owner. Tom brought the whole family. It definitely had potential, with four lakes surrounded by thick forest, in a rustic setting of the Missouri backwoods.

Tom recalls, "It was a mess. No one had mowed it. Garbage cans, beer cans, and paper were everywhere. It was just run-down, but no one lived there."

After much discussion with Hoyt, the owner, and with his family, Tom decided to form a partnership with Hoyt and a couple of other investors to buy the property.

Tom says, "I left school, which was probably my downfall. I should not have left school. I left thinking I was going to build a Bible camp."

Tom went all-in on the project. He was the onsite managing partner, spending hours of hard labor cleaning up the land, chopping, shoveling, and raking. He also enlisted the aid of a local Boy Scout Troop, negotiating an arrangement where they could come out for free camping and fishing in exchange for cleanup labor. He placed two mobile homes on the property, one for his mother and grandmother, and the other for his family.

With a grin, Tom remembers, "I physically put in a waterline to the pump house, over a hundred and some feet. I put it in by hand, with a shovel!"

The partnership named their new property Rockwood Acres. They installed an entry gate, constructed a small gatehouse, and began to collect usage fees for fishing, camping, and swimming. They sold bait and tackle, food and snacks, swimming and camping supplies.

Tom and Isabelle added the final member to the family during this time, bringing little Thomas Daniel into the world on January 7, 1974. It's no coincidence that the name *Daniel* found its way back into the mix. It started out with *Danny* as a tribute to Tom's dad, John Daniel. In memory of their firstborn child, their last born received that name as a tribute to Daniel Dean.

Tom and Isabelle formed a good friendship with their new Rockwood Acres neighbors, a family whose house was situated right near the entry gate to the property. One of their daughters, Marla, had even taken a job with them to operate the gatehouse. Things were looking very positive for the venture. People loved it. Word got out. Families were increasingly showing up every weekend, and money was coming in.

One day, Tom's partners came out to discuss the business with Tom. They had some bad news. Lloyds of London, their insurance carrier, was preparing to drop their coverage due to the liabilities associated with lake swimming. They were requiring an actual pool with lifeguards. The partnership could not afford to make that investment, so they could no longer allow swimming. The place was reduced to fishing and camping only.

The new policy was devastating because people wanted to swim. Families stopped coming, revenue tanked, and eventually the only people showing up were revelers looking for a place to smoke, drink, and skinny-dip.

Tom shakes his head and giggles as he recalls a couple of those encounters, "I remember one time a big gang of cars came out at about two or three o'clock in the morning—they were nothing but hippies."

TOM

Tom saw and heard the group enter and drive to the top lake at the back of the property. By the time he got out there, most of the partygoers were already in the water without a stitch of clothing on. He shined his flashlight out into the crowd, and the exchange went something like this:

Tom: "What are you guys doing?"

Hippie Guy: "Just trying to enjoy a swim."

Tom: "Well, I can't allow you all to swim here. We don't have insurance anymore, so you'll have to get out of the water."

Another Hippie Guy: "C'mon, man! We've been coming out here for years. We aren't hurting anybody."

Tom: "I understand that, and I'm sorry, but I still can't let you swim here."

As some of the gals began to leave the water, one hollered at Tom.

Hippie Gal: "Are you going to turn off that light?"

Tom (with a sly grin): "I'd rather not!"

Frustrated, the girls exited the water as Tom saw way more than he had expected to see that night! Tom continued to try and talk the rest of them out of the water but realized he was in a compromising position. He was just one guy with nothing more than a flashlight, confronting at least half a dozen revelers who were likely under the influence.

After some more back-and-forth discussion, Tom relented and said, "Well, you guys can do what you want tonight, but after tonight, that's it. No more, okay?"

Thankfully they agreed, and Tom ended the exchange with a lighthearted remark, "But I'll tell you one thing: if you get in that water"—and they all stopped—"you're gonna get wet!"

They all laughed, and that was the end of it.

The other encounter that Tom describes was not quite as pleasant. One day a small group of four or five bikers came rambling in. Tom heard the rumble of the motorcycles and looked out to see the group of guys and gals drive around the locked, gated entry, park their bikes, and prepare for midday skinny-dip. Tom rushed down there and stood between them and the shore with his back to the water. He explained the insurance situation to the group and that they couldn't swim.

The bold one of the group quipped, "We've been coming here long before you came around, and we're going swimming today."

Tom responded flatly, "No, you're not. You can't swim here, and that's just how it is."

At that moment, the biker guy took off in a full sprint toward the water, thinking he could just bull his way through. Tom reacted instinctively, drawing upon the high school football skills he had honed as a young man running hundreds of head-to-head tackle drills. Tom executed a textbook, linebacker-style tackle on the guy. Down he went in a tumble of grass and dirt. Tom immediately put a headlock on the biker dude, dragged him back to the group, arms flailing, and pushed him into his motorcycle. The group stood there in state of shock, stunned at what they had just witnessed.

"You got a lot of nerve, one guy against five!" shouted the bold one.

Full of adrenaline and fire in that moment, Tom shouted right back, "And you've got a lot of nerve messing with one guy you know nothing about!"

In a surreal moment of silence, Tom began to realize his situation. He was indeed just one guy in the midst of several. As the bold one began to step forward for round 2, his girlfriend grabbed him by the shoulder and pleaded with him to let it go and leave. Fortunately, he did. They all jumped on their bikes and peeled out of there. As

Tom turned to head back to the house, he realized how narrowly he had just escaped a beating.

"That was a dumb thing I did!" he mumbled to himself.

Chapter Ten

Carol's Story

In January of 1975, while Tom and his family were living on the Rockwood Acres property, he received some news from his sister Carol about their father. John Daniel had passed away from a heart attack. It came as no surprise to Tom that the day had come. It was just a couple years before that he had walked out on John at the hospital while he was recovering from his first heart attack. The story of how he died was also not very surprising to him.

Just a few weeks before, John had undergone open-heart surgery. They had installed a pacemaker. Severely weakened from the procedure, John struggled through the recovery. As with most people going through that ordeal, the doctors laid down all sorts of life-altering rules about diet and activity. When he told them he wanted to go back to the Wyoming ranch to recover (his boyhood home), the doctors told him, "No way." The delicate calibration of the pacemaker would have to be closely monitored and slowly adjusted for the altitude changes, or it would kill him. John's stubbornness kicked in. There was no way he was going to listen to that bull.

Tom recalls, "As soon as he was released, and was able, he hopped in the car and drove straight through from Pekin to Wyoming. He sat down in a rocking chair to watch his last mountain sunset and died right there on the porch."

TOM

Plans were in motion for Tom's siblings to come to his Rockwood Acres home so they could all ride to the funeral together in a van. The funeral was in Cody, Wyoming, over one thousand miles away. That would be quite a trip on any day, but with four siblings and their spouses, eight adults, all crammed into a single vehicle, crossing a thousand miles of countryside, in January, there was reason for concern. The trip would be leading them northwest into mountain country, where winter weather could quickly become very dangerous.

The group of six arrived at Rockwood Acres: Carol and Terry, Tim and Kathy, Til and Glenda. They got settled in for an afternoon visit and began to make plans for an early morning start the next day. Tom was in the kitchen visiting with family as Isabelle prepared a meal for everyone, when all of a sudden, Tom heard his sister let out a bloodcurdling scream.

Tom shouted, "What was that!" But everyone acted as if they hadn't heard a thing.

Tom leaped to his feet and ran to the guest room at the back of the house where Carol was. He knocked loudly on the door, calling out to Carol. She opened the door to find her brother with a bewildered look on his face.

"Are you okay!" he exclaimed.

Carol replied, "Yeah, why?"

Tom explained what he had heard and thought maybe she had fallen and hurt herself. With a confused look, she said it wasn't her. Equally confused, Tom proceeded to find the kids all in the house playing safely; he went outside and looked around, and he found no one. Tom felt very weird, but he knew what he had heard.

Tom says, "That night, I had one of those 'Danny dreams,' at four o'clock in the morning, of all times . . . it always seems to happen at four in the morning."

He dreamed of the road trip they were about to take to Wyoming. He saw Carol and his family, all in a car that slid off the road and into a light pole, striking the side right where Carol was sitting.

Tom describes the dream scene, "She was beat up so bad. It was so cold. This blizzard was so bad. There was nobody else on the road for miles. It was just nothing but white and blizzard."

In the dream, Tom was the only one of them who was dressed for the situation, all bundled up in his insulated hunting gear. Carol was bleeding and hurt very badly, so he set off on foot into the storm to find help. He walked and walked, mile after mile, hour after hour, one light pole after another, across a never-ending wasteland of snow and ice, with no help to be found. He gasped himself awake and sat there in a night sweat until he managed to calm himself down and go back to sleep.

As the group sat around the breakfast table that morning preparing to set out on the road, Tom was haunted by the disturbing imagery from that dream. He also remembered vividly how this had happened with Danny, how he had foreseen the accident days before it actually happened. Even his siblings knew that story, because Tom had shared it with them. He decided to speak up and tell Carol about the dream. The brothers got upset, as did Carol, and flatly told Tom they were going to the funeral, like it or not.

Tom relented, said, "That's fine," then proceeded to collect the very same hunting gear that he had seen in the dream. As the group loaded up the car, they noticed Tom had packed his insulated coveralls, boots, hat, and gloves. They asked what he was doing.

Tom said, "We aren't gonna make it. I'm gonna be the only one warm enough to find us some help because I know what's gonna happen."

As he headed for the door, Carol called out, "Wait a minute. You're freaking me out now. I'm not going."

After much debate, some heated words and frustration, the other girls decided to also not go. Tom and Tim backed out too, leaving Tilas the only one still wanting to press on. They all eventually agreed to pool their money and send Til in a small rental car to be the family representative at the funeral, while the rest stayed behind.

Shortly after Til left, his twin brother, Tim, decided to call the Wyoming Highway Patrol for a road report. To his surprise, they reported mild weather in the fifties.

Tom recalls with a grin, "Wow. Now they're really mad at me!"

After many more hours of waiting and worrying, they finally got a phone call from Til. He proceeded to tell them that he was still about one hundred miles away from Cody. He had run into a surprise snowstorm. The roads into Cody were shut down, covered with snow and ice, and hardly anyone was around for miles. He went on to tell them that the car had spun out of control and slid off the road, narrowly missing a light pole. Til sat in the ditch for over three hours before he saw another soul, when a semi finally picked him up and gave him a ride into the next town, leaving the rental car buried in a snowbank.

There was an eerie silence in Tom's Rockwood Acres home that night as the group processed the story about their brother Til. They realized, had the eight people all been in the van, rather than one guy in a small car, the weight difference would likely have been enough to cause them to hit that pole.

Tom recalls, "They didn't even want to talk about it. It was like . . . 'Tom's weird' . . . but I can't help it."

Til was able to hire a plane the next morning for a short flight into Cody to attend the funeral.

Tom concludes the Carol story, "I wish I had known back then when I had that dream about Danny that it was a warning. If I get a dream like that anymore, it's gonna be a warning. I'm gonna tell you what I saw. Okay? You can do what you want with it, but I'm gonna warn you. I've got more of them I'm gonna share in this book. That saved my sister's life, and we knew there was something different about me."

CHAPTER ELEVEN

A Beginning to an End

As revenues continued to spiral down at Rockwood Acres, Tom had to take a janitorial job at the local Corn's Thriftway grocery store to make ends meet. The Rockwood Acres partnership lost an investor, and the remaining three partners began to experience contention as the other two investors were discussing plans for insolvency without including Tom in the conversation. The two eventually offered Tom a buy-out proposal. Tom talked it over with his grandmother Flossie, who had also invested some money into the venture. Tom recognized that this was a life-lesson and that he should have never left school, so they agreed to sell out and accepted the breakeven proposal; time for a new start (again).

In making the decision to leave Rockwood Acres, Tom had already considered what his next move would be. He knew full well that his grocery store job would never be enough to support his four kids. After he had moved the family into a small house on Tenth Street, in the small town of Oak Grove, Missouri, he decided to put some knowledge to use that he had acquired while at Calvary Bible College.

During those years of going to school, one of his part-time jobs was with Faultless Pest Control. Tom had already picked up a few skills in that line of work at his Ace Spray summer job back in Pekin, but Faultless taught him a whole lot more about the pest control business. He decided to try his own hand at it. He put together a few flyers and strategically placed them around town and in neighboring communities, on grocery store bulletin boards, the Laundromat, the post office, etc. The calls began to come in, and TC Pest Control was born. It wasn't very long that the small, start-up company ran into some trouble.

Tom recalls with a chuckle, "My customers were getting a little upset because I wasn't curing their problem. I didn't know that much about the pest control business, but I do know how to make money."

Recognizing that he needed some help, he made a phone call to a man he had met at Faultless. Harold was more than just a guy Tom knew from that job, he was the company owner, a fifty-year veteran of the industry, and the sitting president of the National Pest Control Association.

Tom says, "Harold was the kind of guy you want to learn from. He really knew his business."

There was some sort of a connection that Harold had with Tom because not only did he take Tom under his wing to train him in the business, he gave Tom a full sponsorship! He even came to Tom's home on occasion to enjoy dinner with his family. The two had formed a master-apprentice relationship, and Tom absorbed every bit of knowledge he could from his mentor. Tom spent hours every day, without pay, going out on the job with the Faultless crew to gain valuable hands-on experience. Upon completion of Harold's sponsorship, Tom emerged as an expert in the craft, knowing exactly how to effectively deal with roaches, spiders, ants, termites, and all manner of household pests.

TC Pest Control took off and was eventually renamed to General Lawn and Pest Control. Tom gained notoriety among his customers and peers as the go-to guy for lawn care and pest control services. There weren't many competitors either, and the few who tried didn't last long. General Lawn was king, covering the market region east of the Kansas City Metro area, including the counties of Lafayette, Jackson, and Johnson. Tom began working commercially as well, forming relationships with real estate companies, the post office, and others. Tom's business grew well beyond his expectations, reaching six figures in revenue.

Tom comments, "That was good money for the 1970s. Totally successful. There's no other way to put it."

Tom and Isabelle were invited to church one day by some new friends they had met, Frank and Lois. Isabelle had been suffering from some migraine headaches, so Frank and Lois wanted to pray for their new friends' health. Not one to forget his Christian roots or his belief in divine healing, Tom gladly accepted the invitation. The church wasn't much more than a few families meeting in a garage, but remained an active attendee and drew upon his church experiences in Red Wing and Lone Jack as a music and youth director. Tom had also gained some excellent scriptural knowledge and insight from his studies at Calvary Bible College, which he had also put to work as an assistant pastor.

Just as his new business was blessed with amazing growth and success, so was his work in the church. A year and a half later, that little 6-family church had grown to over 550 people gathering inside a brand-new, fully packed church building. Parents had spread the word, as teens flourished in Tom's Youth Program. The congregation was asking for Tom to speak more often as the assistant pastor. Something about his delivery style, the quality and content of his message, and the scriptural consistency of his sermons kept them coming back, and in growing numbers. Tom's Sunday morning Bible study was so popular that he ran out of space. He had to move into the senior pastor's study room, and eventually outgrew that space as well. People of all ages started to show up—seniors, couples, and the middle-aged. He soon filled the entire right half of the main sanctuary. That is when the troubles began.

The senior pastor, Walter, was fed up with this young hotshot getting all the attention. His small Bible study group of senior citizens paled in comparison to Tom's growing crowd, and it just wasn't right for a senior pastor to be outdone by a lowly assistant, by a measly youth director. Walter hardened his heart toward Tom, and the enemy used that prideful weakness to undo the good work that was happening in that church.

TOM

On one particular Sunday, as Tom was teaching to his group about who the Arabs were and where they fit into the Bible, in came Walter. He walked right up to the front of the room and interrupted Tom. He began to tell all those who were not part of the youth ministry that they had to leave and go be with their own groups.

Tom recalls, "Walter asked me, 'Is this stuff you're teaching what you learned in college?' I said, 'Yes.' 'Well, you're not going to teach it here anymore! We're not that kind of church!' He did that right there in front of everybody."

The enemy was in motion. Not only was his church work under attack, his family was. More specifically, his wife, Isabelle. She was in an emotional turmoil. Little Danny was her firstborn son too, and it ripped her apart on the inside when he died. But there was something else. Something from a time long ago when she was just a young girl, when the father she trusted had violated that trust in the worst of ways. Those who understand this will recognize it as a pain no woman ever fully heals from. The darkness of that old hurt was amplified by the horror of Danny's death, and it became a catalyst for the destruction of Tom and Isabelle's marriage. Tom had known since the early days of their marriage about the truth of what her father had done.

Tom recalls, "I didn't know about it at first. But when I did, it really angered me. It's a sickness beyond sick, and I didn't want her to be anywhere near that guy. Every time we went over there, I could see the sickness in his eyes. So my leaving Pekin was more than just to go meet my dad. It was also to get Isabelle away from her dad. I lived with that all my life because Isabelle wouldn't talk about it. Even though her dad helped me get the Caterpillar job and helped us with the car wreck and all, it was very hard coming back from Red Wing to be around him again. I made sure my kids were never alone with him—ever."

While living at Rockwood Acres, Isabelle had befriended a young woman named Marla. She was the neighbor's daughter, who had worked for the Rockwood Acres partnership operating the entry gate. Isabelle was not that many years older than Marla, so the two related very well to each other. Marla's older sister, Cindy, was killed in an automobile accident during that time, and of course, Isabelle had recently buried her son, so they developed a very strong friendship and bonded over a common theme—the loss of a loved one.

The impact of Cindy's loss was devastating to Marla and her family. Her father turned to alcohol, her mother became estranged and engaged in a bizarre affair with her dead daughter's boyfriend—even marrying the boy. Her siblings went their own way, leaving Marla on her own to sort out the emotional wreckage. So while Tom was pouring himself into Rockwood Acres, Isabelle was drawing closer to Marla. Over time, certain boundaries were crossed, and the two became something more than friends. Tom saw the signs. He knew something was not quite right with that situation, but he was perplexed on what to do about it. All doubts were removed when he caught the two in the act one day.

Tom reflects on it, "I think Isabelle didn't know where the line was, that love and sex were somehow the same thing. I blame her dad for that, because of what he did to her. He definitely blurred the lines for her on that point."

Tom was reeling. He needed help. So he turned to the church—what a perfect setup the enemy had orchestrated. That was just the opportunity Walter had been waiting for to get Tom out of his church, and he fully exploited it. He gathered the elders and the deacons together in a room, along with a church mediator named Ernie. They all converged on Tom. It was Tom versus the church. They scrutinized him, interrogated him, challenging the very notion of what he was implying. To the point of outright anger and disdain, they berated him. How dare he suggest such a thing about Isabelle! One of the elders told Tom he needed to resign and to focus on his family rather than on the ministry.

Tom recalls, "That's how they thought they were gonna get me out."

The elder told Tom to go out and buy a stove, a washer and dryer, and to focus on making his wife happy. Then Ernie came up with a strange tale about how he had supposedly had seen the spirit of God appear in the sanctuary one Sunday descending and ascending repeatedly like an angel upon Isabelle. Tom could hardly believe

TOM

what he was hearing in that moment, but he knew in his heart what was happening. Tom spoke up, and the exchange went something like this:

> Tom: "Okay. I understand now. But I want to ask you one thing, all you people. Have you had even one complaint about me, or the manner of my service and teaching? Did I not serve well?"
>
> Ernie (loudly exclaimed): "That's not the point!"
>
> Tom (turning his attention directly upon Walter): "I don't really think, Walter, that you brought all of this together. It was *all* of us. It was a team that built this church in a year and a half."
>
> Walter: "God did it."
>
> Tom: "God uses people, Walter."
>
> Walter: "We want you to resign."
>
> Tom (returning his attention to the larger group): "Okay. If that's what you all want, fine. But I want you to know why I've decided to do that. My wife's heart has left me for someone else."

At that moment, the real enemy was revealed, stirring up a hateful wrath in Ernie so ugly that Tom saw it clearly for what it was. The crazed man clenched both fists, slammed the table with all his might, leaped to his feet with so much haste that his chair was knocked over behind him with a loud clang, and he shrieked, "You get on that pulpit Sunday, and you disgrace yourself, and leave this church!"

Tom knew instantly that all of Ernie's talk about seeing the spirit of God was nothing more than a show. It was a ploy, designed to add more pressure on Tom to resign. It was a lie. Tom walked out, accepting that fate.

When Sunday came, it was evident that not Walter, not the elders, not the deacons, not a single one of them had said a word about Tom's resignation to anyone. It was another setup to make certain that Tom would be disgraced in the pulpit. Tom had anguished all week over this moment. What would he say? How could he divulge such a tawdry tale to a church congregation? What about the kids? This would be a devastating truth for his innocent children . . . the rumors, the reputation, the ugliness of it all.

As Tom stood there before the people, trembling, they could tell something was not right. Tom's usual confidence, his cheerfulness and spirit-filled personality was not there.

He proceeded to speak, saying, "God said, if there is a reproach in anybody's life, they cannot serve me. There's been a reproach in my family, to the point that I'm going to have to leave this church and resign."

A collective gasp emanated from the sanctuary. In Tom's own words, he recalls the scene with tearful eyes and a broken voice, "So I began to disgrace myself. I had to leave an impression that it was my fault, that it was my affair. I was trembling so bad . . . I kept thinking . . . Walter, Warren, somebody's gotta stop this! Look at what's happening to me! I'm lying, and you know it! They didn't say a word. They let it happen."

Tom stepped down from the stage and made his way to the back pew of the church and sat beside Isabelle. Thankfully, the kids were in Sunday school and were not exposed to that moment. In stunned silence, no one said a word. No one even looked at him, including Isabelle. For the duration of the service, Tom endured the awkward oppression, broken up inside.

With a disgusted frown, Tom recalls, "After all that, Walter had the audacity to call me out to dismiss the congregation in prayer. You could've shot me with a gun at that moment. It was a very short prayer."

Later that day, Tom returned to an empty church to collect his office belongings. He walked out the front entry and closed the double doors behind him, leaned his back up against the church doors, and cried out to God in hurt and despair, "I will *never* attend your church again for as long as I live!"

Tom still tried to deal with the situation between Marla and Isabelle. He tried to talk and pray with them and got nowhere. He was clearly on his own with the ordeal because the church had completely shunned him after that terrible day of public disgrace.

Tom recalls, "It was really getting to me. I was deeply hurt. Not one person from that congregation called. No one wanted to know what really happened. No one said they were praying for me. Nothing! I never did understand that."

He eventually turned to another church for help. He met with Pastor Andrew from the Assembly of God Church and told him the story, asking if he would counsel the women. Andrew knew of Tom's good reputation. He recognized the immense contribution Tom had made to the growth of Walter's church and was frankly shocked that they would let Tom go like that. He agreed to help. After a few counseling sessions, Tom and Andrew met over coffee to catch up.

Andrew came right out and said, "Tom, I can't help you. This thing is so big and so powerful, it's affected my whole family. I can't even preach when I get done talking to them. I can't talk to them anymore. I don't know what you're gonna do."

As time went by, the situation got worse, to the point where Isabelle expressed hatred for Tom and even threatened to go openly public with the true nature of her relationship with Marla.

Tom recalls Isabelle's rant, "She told me they were going to hold hands and walk up and down main street for all to see how much they loved each other. She also made it clear that she was sick and tired of the church . . . that church was always about me, not her."

Tom tried to flee the situation by moving the family away from Oak Grove to the neighboring town of Odessa, but it made no difference. In fact, another event happened around that time that added even more emotional strain on Isabelle. Her father passed away on September 24, 1977. Two days later, strangely on their wedding anniversary, she stood in front of her dad's casket, never able to tell him about how much he had hurt her. He was laid to rest at Lakeside

Cemetery in Pekin, not far from her little Danny, who is also buried there.

At that time, the General Lawn and Pest Control business was the one bright spot in Tom's mixed-up life. The work kept coming in. He hired a couple of employees to keep up with the demand, one of which was a man named Jim. Something about Jim attracted Marla, so the whole sordid "Isabelle Marla" situation took on an entirely new dimension as Marla started another affair right under Tom's nose. Isabelle didn't like that development one bit. In fact, she was livid.

In a superbly strange twist of fate, Tom realized that could be a way out. It was fairly obvious that Marla was an easy one to get into bed with, so Tom orchestrated an event to do just that. He set up the timing perfectly. When Isabelle came home one day, she caught them in the act, just as Tom had hoped she would. She went ballistic and threw Marla out immediately. The so-called love affair was over!

Sadly, the damage was done. The hurt ran too deep, the church was no longer a part of their lives, and they could not reconcile all the ugliness that had spoiled their marriage. If that wasn't enough, Tom's business also took a bad turn when a severe drought hit the area. It was so bad that Tom had to sell off the business and declare bankruptcy. He ended up taking a sales job with a wholesale merchandise club called Uniway, later renamed to Nu-Mart. Family life continued to spiral downhill. Tom spent more and more time away at the office while Isabelle drifted further and further away from Tom. The end was near.

To add some insight to what was to come, Isabelle was an aspiring model during that time. Always a beautiful woman, she was especially attractive at that time in her life. She had taken a few modeling classes and had performed some photography sessions. She was a natural. She was tall, slender, with long brown hair, big eyes, high cheekbones, and a knockout smile. Her features were quickly noticed as her photographer circulated her best proofs among his peers. A New York agency was interested, and an opportunity was made available for Isabelle to pursue. This all came together at about the same time as the Marla situation reached a tipping point, so she decided to take a few days to get away from it all and think about this life decision. She went to see her mother in Memphis, along with her four children: Steve, Becky, David, and Tommy. After a few days, she prepared a letter and dropped it in the mail to Tom.

He recalls, "The letter was . . . she wanted to go to New York. She had a chance to be a straw boss. She needed two years off. I was not to do anything . . . 'wait until she gets home so we could talk about it.'"

When Tom read those words, he knew. If she left, she would never come back to Missouri. He was also wise enough to see the meaning behind Isabelle's request for him to not do anything until they spoke. Her plans hinged on working something out with Tom for the children. He recognized this fact and knew he had to act immediately to stop her from running off to New York. He immediately packed up all his clothes and personal belongings and moved out.

Tom says, "When she came back, I was gone. It tore her up. She got to where she hated me. Everything went wrong for her. But she stayed. She loved her kids."

That was the end of Tom and Isabelle. The divorce went through. Tom went away and built a new life for himself in Kansas while Isabelle stayed in Odessa living day to day, working, cooking, cleaning, and caring for the four kids. She pursued some education and landed a receptionist job with the State of Missouri. She eventually met a man and remarried. No one in that little Missouri town ever knew the true story behind what had happened. Tom maintained the image of fault, allowing everyone to blame him while they felt sorry for Isabelle. Even his own children were allowed to believe those things about their father.

In Tom's own words, "I had to leave it that way. I gave no defense, because I had four kids going to school in a very small community. If that had gotten out, it would have destroyed all of them. Instead, it was me everybody hated."

Tom poured himself into his work. He rose to the top at Nu-Mart, making Man of Year. He then left to rebuild his pest control business and started a secondary business called Ceiling Master of Kansas City. He even drove a school bus part-time. Tom drifted far away from God and the church during those years. Consumed by the hurt of losing his family, angry at God for putting all the blame on him, he engaged in one affair after another. He even remarried, only to divorce again after a short time. Tom held on to that hurt for a long time, rebelling against God and his Christian ways.

"I was really upset," Tom remembers. "I became a renegade. I played around. I didn't care. Nobody cared about me, and I didn't care about nobody either. I didn't care about God, and I didn't go to church anymore."

That was Tom's lifestyle over the next few years. In 1986, his oldest son, Steve, graduated from high school and decided to attend a local Kansas City college. In October of that year, Steve moved in with Tom and became a full-time, working college student. Steve moved out on his own a couple years later and was on his way to building his own adult life—one down, three to go.

Chapter Twelve

My Kids Are in Trouble

During Tom's rebellious years, rebuilding his life in Kansas, regrowing his business, and catering to his carnal whims, he eventually met a woman who brought some healing to his heart. Twila was about as gentle and stable as a soul could be, and Tom was drawn to her. They met at a mixed bowling league and soon moved in together. Life was heading in the right direction again for Tom as he aged into his midforties.

One summer night in 1988 as Tom and Twila were sleeping, a strange, yet familiar, feeling came over him. He was jerked out of sleep, gasping and sweating. He was not dreaming nor had he been awakened by a nightmare. He sat there in bed deeply disturbed by something unknown. He noticed the time on the clock—4:00 a.m., always 4:00 a.m. Tom knew something was not right. He had felt this before.

He got up and went to the kitchen for a glass of water, then stepped out onto the back deck into the cool night breeze. Tom gazed up into the star-filled sky toward the little Missouri town where his kids were. Suddenly, a haunting sensation of peril filled his spirit. It was as if an audible voice filled his mind, "My kids are in trouble."

He immediately raised both hands toward God and prayed one of the sincerest prayers of his life, "God, I don't know what's going on, but please, don't let my children die."

Almost instantly, a wave of relief came over Tom. He knew his prayer had been received, so he went back to bed. Morning came, and the phone rang. It was Isabelle. His two youngest boys, David and Tommy, were both in jail on charges of armed robbery.

Things were looking pretty grim for the boys. David had just recently turned sixteen, so the prosecutor wanted to try him as an adult. He was facing a very long prison sentence. At fourteen, Tommy would most certainly be locked away in juvenile detention for the next four years of his life, and possibly more. Neither Tom nor Isabelle had the money to afford a high-powered attorney to defend their kids, so they opted for the public defender.

As the court date approached, Tom was faced with a dilemma. He was badly hurt from a work-related injury and had just gone through back surgery a few days before the boys' court appearance. With a fused lumbar, confined to a wheelchair, and in serious pain, Tom and Twila went to the court proceeding against his doctor's advice. Isabelle and her new husband, Larry, along with Tom's daughter Becky, had arrived at about the same time. They were ushered into a room where Larry and Twila were not permitted. It was a private meeting, for family only. Alone in that room were his two boys. They all sat down—David, Tommy, Becky, Tom, and Isabelle (Steve, the working college student, could not arrange to be there that day). Tom looked across the table at David.

> David: "Look. Look around, Dad!"

> Tom (looking around, he wasn't sure what David was referring to): "What do you see, David?"

> David (overcome by emotion, tears flowing and voice breaking): "For the first time in years, we're together as a family. It was worth it!"

> Sobbing deeply, all joined in crying.

Tom (choking back his own tears): "David. You're in a lot of trouble."

David: "I don't care. We're together."

Tom: "David. I made a mess out of my life, and I'm sorry. I hope you can forgive me. I only know one person who can help us now. Jesus. I'm gonna ask him for his help. Will you pray with me?"

They joined hands and prayed.

With great emotion, Tom recalls the moment, "I prayed a prayer like you wouldn't believe. The Spirit of God flowed through me as I cried for forgiveness and mercy."

The family stayed in the room and waited. They were scheduled for a one o'clock proceeding, but it was after two.

Finally, the attorneys came in and apologized for the delay, saying, "The judge has not come out of his chambers yet, so we don't know what's going on. He's never late."

Another half hour ticked by, and the judge was still in his chambers. The attorney had even knocked on the judge's door, but he didn't answer. It was almost three o'clock when the attorneys came in again and suggested moving into the court room. At that moment, the judge came into the private family room and exchanged introductions. David was sitting in between his mom and dad at that moment. The judge walked up behind David and rubbed the boy's shoulders.

He leaned over to look into David's eyes and said, "What is a good-looking boy like you doing in a mess like this?"

David broke down into an emotional mess. He hugged his mom and dad, sobbing, weeping, holding on to a small glimmer of hope for his family to be reunited, as he cried out to the judge about how sad and hurt he was with the divorce.

When David finally got it all out and calmed down, the judge spoke, "I've been a judge for sixty years. Not once did I ever have to pray to figure out what I'm going to do. I paced the floor, and I prayed to God, asking him what he wanted me to do with you boys, and I still didn't know what to do. Now that I've talked to you and seen your face, I've made up my mind."

He turned to the attorneys and announced that *both boys* would be tried as juveniles. The prosecutor erupted in protest, but the judge silenced him immediately.

"We're going to give these boys another shot at life! Now shut up and let's get on with it!" proclaimed the judge.

The trial was conducted, and David was scheduled to go to juvenile detention in St. Louis. Tom's heart sank, because the reputation of that particular facility in St. Louis was very bad. Everyone knew that was the worst place to send a kid. David would surely come out of there a hardened criminal. The attorneys made every effort to arrange for him to go to the Watkins Mill Boys' Home, but there were no openings. Once again, Tom went into fervent prayer, pleading God for a door to be opened for David.

The decision for Tommy was bit more involved. Since he was younger, he had the option to be released into parental custody. Isabelle adamantly proclaimed that Tommy would be far worse with his dad, but in a bizarre contradiction of motherhood, she also stated that he couldn't come to live with her. She was apparently abandoning her son to the system.

With a perplexed look on his face, Tom recalls the moment, "She shocked everybody when she said that. She came right out and told the judge she hoped they put him away for life! I couldn't believe such a thing would ever come out of her mouth."

Tom quickly lobbied to have Tommy placed with him and Twila, but that presented the judge with a two-part problem: (1) they lived in Kansas and (2) they were not married.

When the judge explained that he couldn't place Tommy with them for those reasons, Twila immediately spoke out, saying, "But we're going to get married!"

That caught Tom completely off guard. He knew that Twila was not the marrying kind. In fact, she had told him up front when they started dating that marriage was not in the cards. But he was not about to bring that up in such a tense moment, so he just rolled with it!

The judge's attitude changed in an instant. He excitedly leaned forward. "Really? If you get that marriage done and you bring me the paperwork, that will change everything!"

The court proceeding ended, and arrangements were made for Tommy to go to the Shiloh Boys Home until the wedding. Tom and Twila made the long drive back to Kansas, uncertain and scared for David's future. They also discussed her notion of marriage. They agreed that as soon as Tommy got out that they would annul the marriage.

The next morning, Tom received a call from the attorney. "You're not going to believe this! Someone was just released from Watkins Mill, and they are going to take David in!"

Praise the Lord! David was at Watkins Mill until he was eighteen. Tom and Twila were married, and within a few months, Tommy was released from Shiloh to come live with them in Kansas. True to their word, Tom and Twila annulled the marriage soon after.

Tom praises Twila, saying, "She's my friend to this day. Wherever she goes, she'll always be remembered by me and my children because she saved Tommy."

Tom's back injury and surgery were quite severe, and he had created even more of a problem for himself by going against the doctor's orders to attend the boys' court proceeding so soon after the surgery. Twila was his hero, nursing him back to health over the next few months. Tom recalls a particular situation from his back recovery that remains with him to this day.

In Tom's own words, "My days as a prodigal all changed in 1988 when I severely injured my back. I thought I'd never walk again. The physical therapy was beyond pain. Even with parallel bars, it was all I could do to take even one step. One day I was lying in bed, home alone, when I tried to get up. I rolled over and fell right out of the bed onto my knees right in front of a chair that was beside the bed. There I was in a kneeling position with my chest across the chair, unable to get up. I could barely lift my head. I was in unbearable pain with back spasms. So I began to pray, 'Dear God, please help me. Please heal my back. Please let me walk again. I promise I will never do wrong again.'"

Tom's prayer was answered, but it took some time. Twila finally got home from work and found Tom three hours later. Many more difficult months went by, but he eventually recovered fully and went back to work. He never forgot the promise he made to God in those three hours of hell. Tom will be the first to tell you he is far from perfect and still made plenty of mistakes after that day, but never again did he act out as he did in the 1980s, womanizing and such. Tom's heart was truly changed that day.

CHAPTER THIRTEEN

God Answered

It was the mid-1990s when Tom and Twila parted ways. He settled into a new life, with a new wife, at a pretty little place in rural Kansas called Tanglewood Lakes. Nestled in the woods of southeastern Kansas, Tanglewood was a pleasant reminder of his younger days at Rockwood Acres. He spent much of his free time doing the same laborious tasks as he had twenty years before—cutting, clearing, burning, beautifully landscaping the property into a private lakeside resort. That kind of mindless work was a labor of love for Tom, therapeutic in its own way. The same old pickax he had used for thirty years was still digging up roots and rocks like an old pro.

Tom's Tanglewood home was perched on a slope overlooking the lake where he spent many hours relaxing on the deck sipping coffee and watching nature. A boat dock stretched over the water where he also spent many hours with a fishing pole in his hand, occasionally accompanied by his little grandson Scott (Steve's firstborn).

Tom's youngest son, Tom Jr., was a young man of nineteen at that time. He was in a relationship with a much older woman who had a few children from a previous marriage. The woman was in her forties, and Tom Jr. wanted to marry her. Tom Sr. knew the marriage would not work. He counseled Tom Jr. many times against it, but he was determined to go his own way on the matter. Tom relented, realizing that he wouldn't be able to sway the headstrong youth. He used to be one after all. He only asked his son for the following things:

1. Go to three church services of his choice before the wedding
2. Use an ordained minister for the ceremony
3. Accept couples counseling from that minister prior to the wedding

Tom Jr. went to three random church services as his father had asked. When he returned to speak with his dad about it, Tom asked, "What did they say?"

Tom Jr. replied, "Dad, you wouldn't believe it, but every sermon was about marriage."

Tom recalls that encounter with a grin, "That's another one of those things that can't be a coincidence. I had no way of knowing what church would be talking about matrimony, but God did, and he sent Tommy right where he needed to go."

Regardless, Tom Jr.'s stubborn mind was unchanged, and he forged ahead with his wedding plans. As the day drew near, Tom Jr. confirmed for his dad that he had chosen a preacher for the ceremony. Tom Sr. knew the minister his son had named, so he was about as comfortable as he could get with the notion, even though he knew in his heart that the wedding was a mistake.

They decided to have the wedding at Tom's Tanglewood Lakes home, at a beautiful spot near the boat dock under a giant shade tree overlooking the water. Decorations were hung, guests showed up, friends and family joined, and the minster arrived to take his position for the rendering of the vows. When Tom Jr. and his bride arrived, Tom took notice of the minister's face. It was very clear that this was the first time he had ever seen the nineteen-year-old together with his forty-something fiancée.

Tom quietly asked the minister, "Did you not counsel this couple and bless their union?"

The man briefly stared back into Tom's eyes. In that moment of silence, he could see the panic in the minister's eyes. Tom simply exhaled a sigh of disgust and walked away as the ceremony began to start. The ball was already rolling down the mountain, so the minister just rolled with it.

The traditional statement was made by the minister before beginning the vows, "If there is anyone here who has reason to oppose this couple's marriage, let them speak now or forever hold your peace."

In that moment, three acorns fell from the giant oak tree above them, and each one landed squarely upon the minister's open Bible with a very audible *thump, thump, thump.*

Shocked, the minister looked up and said out loud, "Wow!"

An awkward moment of silence went by as the audience wasn't quite sure what had just happened. But Tom knew. God just answered.

"I think the minister knew too. He just didn't have the guts to put a stop to it right there in front of everybody. It was like God said, 'Are you nuts!'" Tom says, chuckling at the memory.

It is a funny afterthought looking back from twenty years later, but for the young Tom Jr., it was not funny at all living through the turmoil of those next few years of life. The marriage was a disaster. Tom Jr. endured a wife sickened by anger, bitterness, and alcohol. He became her preferred target for all kinds of mental, emotional, and outright physical abuse. They divorced after only a few years.

CHAPTER FOURTEEN

A Voice from the Closet

As you read this book, you probably know by now what Tom's siblings had recognized so long ago from Danny's and Carol's stories; there's something different about Tom. His dreams and visions, the eerie feelings and strange encounters he experiences, are all testaments to what Tom believes is a life used by God to accomplish his will. Perhaps you have an unusual set of events in your own life that speaks to the same thing? This next story seems to take Tom to the next level.

In the late 1990s, Tom had settled into a small house in the rural southeastern Kansas town of LaCygne, affectionately called the City of Swans by locals. He continued to operate his pest control business, servicing communities all across the surrounding counties, including Linn, Miami, Johnson, and occasionally across the Missouri state line into Bates or Cass county. He continued his interests in outdoor sports and hunting. He got involved in competitive archery with area leagues and was even a winner at several regional and state-level meets. With his kids all grown up at that time, he was an empty nester living alone. He had just recently ended his fourth marriage.

On one particular autumn night around Thanksgiving time, Tom was sleeping soundly in his little Kansas house. He heard a deep voice call out, "Tom." It was loud enough to wake Tom from his

TOM

slumber. He propped himself up, rubbed his eyes, and looked at the clock—4:00 a.m.

Laughing, Tom tells the story, "Same thing! Four o'clock in the morning! I don't know what it is about four o'clock in the morning, that must've been the time when Jesus finally came down to the disciples, and they were all asleep in the garden!"

Tom lay there in the darkness for a few moments, listening intently for the voice. There was only silence. He passed it off as a weird dream and lay back down. A few moments went by, and Tom was just beginning to drift off to sleep again, when the voice called out again, louder, "Tom!" He instantly sat up, knowing full well what he had just heard.

He thought to himself, *Oh my gosh! Someone's in my house!*

He got up, turned on some lights, looked all around the house, checked all the doors, and looked out the windows to check for prowlers.

Tom recalls, "I went outside and looked in my shop, I went all around my house—there was nobody there."

He went back inside and closed up, turned off the lights, and sat down on the edge of his bed, thinking, *I know I heard it. Was I dreaming? Am I still dreaming?*

As he collected himself and prepared to go back to bed, he peered into the open closet at the foot of his bed. On any other night, he could see into the closet fairly well from the splash of light that filtered through the window from the streetlamp outside, but not that night. Instead, what he saw inside the closet was a cloudy haze, like an empty room.

From the haze came a clearly audible voice, saying, "Tom. Get your life together. Go to your children and tell them, I'm coming soon."

In the blink of an eye, the image was gone. There in the closet hung his clothes, his shoes were on the closet floor—like any other night. He sat there for a moment, processing the encounter, feeling a combined sense of awe and wonder at the same time.

Tom tries to explain the sensation like this, "When the voice called my name, it was like it always knew me. It was like I had always existed, like it had always been a part of me. It was eternal. There was no fear, no anger, it just felt like a very dear friend who missed me."

Later that day as he was making the long drive to Kansas City for work, he couldn't stop thinking about what had happened. It was as if a quiet confidence filled his heart, giving him an overwhelming sense of assurance that all his prayers would be answered. He felt like he could ask for anything, and it would be done.

Tom prayed these words, "I think you're talking to me, Lord, so this is what I ask. When my time comes, and I have to stand before you, I want to know that I am saved, redeemed, and born again. I want to see my name written in the Lamb's Book of Life, and under my name, I want to see the names *Daniel Dean, Steven Scott, Rebecca Jane, David James,* and *Thomas Daniel,* and that we will all live together in the house of the Lord forever. That's what I want, Lord."

That began a new nightly ritual for Tom, praying for his children. It reignited his passion for the Gospel. He began to share his testimony on a regular basis with area churches. He shared Danny's story, Steve's story, Odie's and Dale's stories, and more. He got his life together as he was commanded, and his relationships with his adult children were greatly improved over the years.

Chapter Fifteen

Something in Her Head

It was sometime after his "voice from the closet" experience, while living in LaCygne, Kansas, that Tom had another strange experience. Was it a dream? Was it a vision?

Tom says, "It just seemed real. I think it was a dream, because when I woke up, it was four in the morning, again!"

Tom had never been inside the Kansas City apartment that Isabelle was living in at that time, but he described it with uncanny accuracy as he shared this dream with his son Steve, who had been there many times.

In the small kitchen, Isabelle stood there, warming a pot of coffee, as their four kids were gathered around talking, smiling, and enjoying one another's company. Tom was on the other side of the kitchen wall sitting on a barstool, watching the scene unfold through a cutout portion of the wall.

Tom recalls with a cracked voice, "It was hard to speak. It was so good to be there. I'm home with my family."

With his hands folded under his chin, elbows on the bar, he soaked up the moment, listening to the sounds of that happy moment. Isabelle came over to Tom and rested her arms on the bar top. She looked right into Tom's eyes and leaned in.

Isabelle: "I have a very serious injury on my head."

Tom: What do you mean?"

Isabelle (turning her head, she pointed to a spot near the back of her head): "What do you see?"

Tom: "There's nothing there, Isabelle."

Isabelle: "Yes, there is. Take a look. Feel it."

As Tom reached out to feel the spot, Isabelle grabbed his hand, opened it up, and gently rested her cheek upon his open palm and softly smiled up at him. That moment seemed to last forever.

In his own words, holding back the tears, Tom says, "I was scared to death for her to move, or me to move. That was the most precious thing. Tears rolled down my eyes as she just laid her cheek in my hand. It was so beautiful."

Abruptly, Isabelle snapped upright and said, "Well, I gotta go!"

With a chuckle, Tom recalls, "That' just how she used to talk in real life—'I gotta go!'"

They all began to leave the room, circling behind Tom on the way out. In desperation, Tom tried with all his might to speak out, "Please don't go!" but he was unable to talk. One by one they passed by, through a set of Old West–style bar doors (uniquely similar to a pair that hung in the Odessa home for years). A distinct slapping sound was made as each one of his family walked out. The final door slap sounded, and Tom sat there sobbing deeply, tears streaming down his face, in one of the deepest emotional pains he had ever known, reliving the loss of Isabelle and his children.

He cried out to God, "Why couldn't I stop them!"

Just then, a sound came from the kitchen. Tom quickly tried to regain his composure, wiping his eyes, and looked up to behold an amazing figure. There stood a man, tall, in his thirties, with the most beautiful shroud of light he had ever seen emanating from the man's hair.

The figure spoke, "Can we put Tom aside for a minute?"

TOM

The man stood there, fiddling with a suspender strap on his shoulder, and asked, "Do you want to know what's really amazing?"

Tom sat there speechless, in awe of the sight, petrified, unable to move or speak. In his heart, Tom knew he was seeing the light of God.

"For all the stupid and crazy things we do in life, we're still loved. It's not mine to tell you your future. But instead of looking for love, give it, and love will find you."

Tom pondered the message, looking down. As he did, the figure began to walk out in the same manner as his family had just done, walking behind him toward the bar-style doors. In that instant, a rush of recognition filled Tom's mind. That voice. He knew that voice. It was Isabelle's dad!

He quickly turned to stop the man to talk some more, but no one was there. He darted his head all around, stood up, and looked around, but he was gone.

Several weeks after that dream vision, Tom continued to be bothered by it. He decided to take a trip to Pekin. He made his usual rounds, visiting family and old friends, and as always, to little Danny's grave site. But Tom had other motivations for being there that day. He found himself standing in the rain, looking down at the grave of Isabelle's father.

He sat down on the wet ground with his back against the headstone and spoke these words out loud, "Thomas, I don't know if that was you at my house that day or what. But I know one thing, it brought me here. I kept Isabelle away from you because of what you did to her. I hated you for it. I hated what you did to your daughter. But I know now that God wants me to forgive you. Obviously, he has forgiven you, because I saw the light of God in you."

Tom says, "The animosity and hurt that was in me toward Isabelle ended that day. I'm sharing this story not only for the truth of forgiveness, but that there really was something in her head that took her life. She told me about it in that dream, but I didn't know what it was."

True indeed. Isabelle was diagnosed in 2005, years after that dream, with a rare and debilitating neurological condition called

Cerebella Atrophy. On October 30, 2013, she succumbed to the degenerative effects of that disease. That is another one of those stories that Tom cannot write off as a coincidence. He knows that God has always been up to something in his life. With his children now grown, and their children growing up to become parents, they must learn that the success of life is the retention of God in your life—and to share it with others.

Chapter Sixteen

Love Finds Tom

Tom continued to run his pest control business for many years from his little house in LaCygne, Kansas. He still enjoyed hunting and competitive archery. He continued to share his testimony with local churches and youth groups, using the Dale, Odie, and Steve stories to reach people's hearts. He was even invited to speak on one Father's Day and used his experiences with his own dad that resonated with many young men who struggled in the relationships with their fathers.

Tom recalls a cherished memory from sharing his testimony, "That night, eighteen kids came forward. There wasn't a dry eye in the room. One of the things I emphasized was that it is not as important knowing I was ever loved by my father, but that I loved him. That's how it is with God the Father. He loves us no matter what we do."

In his LaCygne days, Tom enjoyed an occasional visit from his adult children, and his youngest, Tom Jr., had joined him in 1999 to help run the business. His life was on the right track again. Coryell & Sons Pest Control had formed a partnership with a local real estate firm to provide termite inspections as part of the home sales they processed. On a regular basis, Tom came to the office to hand-deliver his inspection reports. Over a period of three years doing that, he had developed a good friendship with a particular person at the firm, Debbie. One particular evening, after a long day of running his routes, Tom arrived home to find a message on his answering machine from Debbie.

The message went something like this: "Hi, Tom. My mother asked me today if I knew of a good exterminator. She's been having a bug problem, so I told her about you. If you could help her out, I'd appreciate it. By the way, she's single and good-looking!"

Tom recalls, "That was some compliment coming from a daughter. She must have really liked me!"

Tom tried to make arrangements for his son to stop by and check out the issue, but he was unable to make it. So Tom decided to tend to the matter himself.

Tom says, "That's when I met Judy. We immediately liked each other and started dating."

One of those dates included a nice dinner at Tom's home in LaCygne. After dinner, Judy noticed a piano that Tom had in the room, and she asked who played it. Tom explained to Judy how he had a natural talent ever since he was a little kid to play by ear.

He told the story where he had tried to take some lessons as a child when his grandma Flossie noticed his talent. He was naturally gifted, so it seemed only natural to try and develop those skills. But after only a few lessons, he had to quit because it was simply not working for him trying to learn the mechanics of music reading, keys, scales, and all that comes with learning music. He went back to playing for fun whatever tune he could carry in his head, and he continues to play that way today.

That night with Judy, he sat down in front of the piano and played a few of his favorite old tunes, like "Ragtime," "The Old Rugged Cross," and a few other Gospel hymns. Judy's face lit up with joy. She was quite impressed. Tom had no idea how much she enjoyed the piano. That inspired him to want to play something really special for her. From times passed, he knew there were occasions when an amazingly beautiful tune would pour out of him unexpectedly that he was unable to reproduce the next day. He paused for a moment and silently lifted a private prayer request for one of those inspirations.

Tom describes the moment, "I looked at the keys, plunked a few, and thought, *Well, that wasn't what I was hoping for.* Then all of the sudden, a song began to play in my head. That was all I needed, because if I can hear a song, I can play it. I began to play. It was so beautiful that I got goose bumps on my arms, the hairs on my neck were standing up, and I remember thinking to myself, *Man, this is really good!*"

He finished the piece and turned to ask Judy what she thought. But before he could speak the sentence, he saw Judy slumped to the floor, tears streaming down her face, smiling from ear to ear. It was clear. Tom's request to play her something special was answered in a big way.

Tom laughs out loud at the memory, saying, "Three weeks later, we were married, and she bought me a new piano! I played for her every night!"

His tired old hands and fingers don't play as well, or as often, as they used to, but you can still hear the happy sounds of piano music emanating from his Tennessee home every so often, and Judy is sure to be listening intently for his next beautiful inspiration.

Chapter Seventeen

Helen's Story

WHEN TOM WAS a young teenager in the early 1960s, one of his favorite places to spend time was Spring Lake. Just a few miles outside his hometown of Pekin, Illinois, he had been going there for years with his brothers, friends, and various family members. Swimming, fishing, boating, and all forms of lake recreation were, and still are, one of Tom's great joys.

During that time, he had met a pretty young girl at school named Pat. Pat was Tom's first love—puppy love, he calls it.

As luck would have it, she lived by Spring Lake. Tom spent many hours visiting his girlfriend and enjoying the lake with her family.

Tom says, "Her parents, Helen and Junior, couldn't believe that Pat and I didn't get married. They thought for sure that's what was going to happen. They treated me like one of their own all those years."

Nearly forty years later, Tom decided to make a visit to his old hometown. His adult daughter Becky had made arrangements to take some time off of work to join her dad on the trip. Tom wanted to show her the lake he had spent so much time around as a kid. As he was driving around one day pointing out various places from his memory, they spotted an old country church named Isabel Church. Of course, they stopped and snapped a photo!

TOM

As Tom continued his trip down memory lane with his daughter, he told her about Pat, Helen, and Junior. He wanted to visit them and eventually found the old street they had once lived on so long ago. They were still there! In fact, Junior was standing on the corner that very day selling produce!

As they stood there talking about old times and catching up, he asked about Helen. "She's inside," Junior said.

As Junior and Becky continued to talk, Tom went inside to see Helen.

Tom describes the scene, "Helen was sitting on the sofa, on a cushion, with her legs crossed, both hands down by her side, and with an oxygen mask on. She looked pretty bad. She could hardly breathe. She had emphysema."

Tom asked her what was wrong, and she told him, "Remember how I used to always say 'there's another nail in my coffin' whenever I lit a cigarette? Well, it's got me, Tom. It's got me."

As he stood there in that moment, he experienced something strange, yet uniquely familiar. He had felt this kind of thing before. A vision had taken form in his mind. It was an image of Helen, as if she were pictured on a baseball card. The card image slowly lifted from her body then quickly shot upward to the ceiling and disappeared.

Tom perceived the experience to mean that Helen's spirit was preparing to leave her body. There was a sense of urgency in his heart to immediately witness to Helen. He had no idea if she was saved or had ever heard the Gospel message. Just as he was about to speak on the matter, Junior and Becky came in.

The four of them spent the next hour or so enjoying a nice visit, reminiscing about the good ol' days. Tom and Becky drove back to Pekin to his sister's house, but he still felt a pull of urgency in his soul over the vision he had seen with Helen. He left Becky with Carol and drove right back to Spring Lake to find Helen's daughter, Pat, to discuss the matter.

Tom recalls, "I knew where she lived because I had visited her before. She married a guy named Ed, and we were pretty good friends. They're Christians, really good Christians."

They sat there for a while on the front porch visiting, and Tom began to talk about Helen.

Tom: "Pat. What's wrong with Helen?"

Pat: "She's dying, Tom. For two years, she's sat on that sofa. She won't go to her bed, she doesn't cook or clean house, she does nothing but sit on that sofa and rock."

Tom: "I remember you telling me that you and Ed are involved in church."

Pat: "Oh yeah, we go to Bible study and everything."

Tom (trying to get a sense of how she might perceive the vision experience he was about to share with her): "A fundamental church?"

Pat: "Yes."

Tom: "I saw something while I was there today. I looked into your mom's eyes, and I saw her spirit leave her."

Pat: "What do you mean?"

Tom (described the vision, with a sense of urgency in his voice): "I want you and Ed to go to your mom *today* and give her the salvation story and lead her to Jesus Christ."

Pat asked Tom to go with them. He wanted to, but when he considered how the moment was interrupted when Junior had come into the house after Tom saw the card image vision, he felt a strong sense that God had another plan for that situation.

TOM

He explained to Pat, "This is not for me to do. It's for you and Ed. And you'll retain this. What you're about to do, for the rest of your life, you'll be glad you did."

Pat was unsure how to even share the salvation story, let alone lead her own mother to Christ. Tom practiced the method with her that he had learned so long ago from Pastor Don, the same one he had used with Dale and many others over the years.

Once Pat had got the sequence down, she asked, "How soon do you think I should go?"

Tom responded with emphasis, "*Now.*"

"Right now?" she asked.

With Tom's emphatic response, "Yes, right now!"

Pat began to share his sense of urgency. They said their goodbyes, and Tom walked out to his car to leave. He looked back to see Pat standing on the porch. Tom locked eyes with her, firmly pointed to the ground, and mouthed one silent word, "Now." She turned and went inside as Tom got into his car and left.

Tom had no idea how that situation turned out. He simply didn't maintain close contact with them. Nearly two years later, he found himself back in Pekin visiting family. He wanted to visit his old friends again, so he drove out to the old familiar Spring Lake road where Helen and Junior lived. It was empty, and some people he didn't know were in the yard.

He continued on to Pat and Ed's. As they sat there visiting again, just as they had two years before, Tom asked Pat if she had followed through on what he had asked. She told Tom that she chickened out to do it alone and had called her pastor instead, who gladly offered to join her. Pat had also called several family members from the area, and they all showed up at the house to be there with Helen that day.

Tom knew that most of the family members who showed up were not very godly people. Most had probably never set foot inside a church, let alone listened to a preacher share the Gospel message. Tom realized at that moment why God had put it in his heart to not go that day.

Pat described a beautiful scene where the whole family was gathered around Helen as she sat on her sofa cushion, listening intently with labored breath through the oxygen mask. They all heard the good news of Jesus Christ and watched in amazement as Helen rose to her feet, removed the mask from her face, and kneeled beside the pastor to pray the sinner's prayer. Praise God!

Pat continued the story, saying, "Tom, you're not going to believe this, but she never did put her mask back on. She got up and fixed coffee for everybody. That night she went to her own bed and slept next to her husband for the first time in two years. She got up and fixed breakfast for her guests the next day. She stood at the sink singing 'Amazing Grace' while washing dishes."

As Pat told him that story, Tom remembered how much Helen had loved that song. She used to always ask him to play it on the piano as she sang along. Helen went to her own bed again that night with her husband and passed away peacefully in her sleep.

In Tom's own words, "That story gives me goose bumps, even now. It's what this book is all about. These are some of the stories I want to share with you, because it's no coincidence. I saw something happen, and God did the rest. But it wasn't just to get Helen saved, God gave the message to her entire family."

Chapter Eighteen

All Things Work Together

July 22 was not always the fun day Tom would have liked it to be growing up. It seemed like his twin brothers or his big sister always had the best birthdays, with lots of guests and great presents, while his were no big deal. But he always had something they didn't; it was the same day as his mom's.

Tom says, "I was born on her birthday. We always had a cake that said Happy Birthday Mom and Tom."

Elinor kept up with Tom's birthday even into adulthood, sending him a card every year without fail. Inside the card was always a dollar bill and a handwritten message quoting her most favorite and beloved passage of scripture, Romans 8:28, "And we know that all things work together for good to them that love God, to them who are the called according to his purpose."

Elinor continued that tradition with her grandchildren. Tom's adult kids share fond memories of the arrival of similar letters—the crisp dollar bill that seemed like it had been freshly printed that day and, of course, her handwritten quote of Romans 8:28. That verse clearly resonated with Elinor. Perhaps it was something she clung to after being so emotionally broken by John and locked away at Bartonville.

In 2007, Tom was living on his rural Kansas property near the small town of Mound City when he received a phone call from his sister Carol. She told him that their mom wasn't doing too well and urged him to make the trip back to Illinois for her birthday. Feeling like it could be her last one, Carol wanted to make it special. Tom knew right away something that would put a big smile on his mom's face.

He called his older twin brothers. The three of them used to play music together. With Tom on the piano, Tim on the trombone, and Til on the cornet, there were many gatherings in years past where they all remembered how much their mom enjoyed their music. Even though it had been nearly forty years since they had played together, the twins agreed to bring their instruments.

Carol made all the arrangements, reserving the room at the nursing home, getting the cake ordered, catering the food, and making sure as many family as possible could be there. It was indeed a special birthday party for Elinor.

Tom says with a smile, "So we all went back there with our instruments, and we had a birthday cake. Guess what it said? Happy Birthday Mom and Tom."

The brothers set up in the room and played just like they had always done so long ago, performing right on key two of Elinor's favorites: "He Touched Me" and "I'd Like to Tell You What I Think of Jesus." They continued to play and sing several more classic hymns for their mom.

Tom recalls, "Every time I'd look out, she was just a smiling and a so happy wrinkled old pruney face!"

In a short period of time, the room was filled with other elderly people from the nursing home singing along, clapping their hands, and tapping their feet to the wonderful old songs they remembered from their past. Even the nursing home staff stopped in to enjoy the performance.

Tom recalls the moment, "I had this feeling come over me. Everybody is here—her brothers, her sisters, children, grandchildren. We're playing, she's happy. That's never happened for Mom before. This is so perfect. I had a feeling like, I don't think I'm ever gonna see my mom like this again. I think this is it."

TOM

They closed the performance with an encore of her favorite song. She sat there smiling, yet crying. What a precious moment. Tom went to his mom, and she held him tight, burying her face in his neck for a long moment.

Still holding on, she looked into Tom's eyes and said, "Tom, I'm not going to be here very long. When I die, please don't cry for me. I'm going to heaven. I know where I'll be, and I'll be there waiting for you."

With a soft voice, Tom describes the moment, "I couldn't help but cry too. I never did get a hug from my mom like that. It was pretty good."

The party concluded, and everyone went back home to their busy lives. A few days later, Tom needed to register a vehicle he had recently purchased. On a Friday afternoon, he found himself stuck in line at the dreaded DMV waiting for his plates and registration. To no one's surprise, he endured a frustrating series of delays and diversions all throughout the long ordeal, including the following:

- When he finally got to the clerk, he realized he had forgotten the money.
- When he came back in, it took a while for the clerk to notice before calling him back up.
- Before they got restarted, she had a priority phone call come in.
- He was then shuffled over to another clerk, who ended up sending him right back.

The clerk finally completed the paperwork, walked over to the stack of new plates, and randomly grabbed a set for Tom. He drove back home and installed the plates, paying no attention to the plate numbers. He stepped back, snapped a photo, and began to inspect the quality of the shot when something caught his eye. The plate number: QRC 828.

An immediate sense of comfort washed over him as he remembered so clearly all those many cards and letters from Mom over the years referencing her favorite verse: Romans, chapter 8, verse 28—

RC 828. It was as if his mom had just placed a reassuring hand on his shoulder to say, "Everything's going to be okay." He wondered if all those crazy delays and diversions at the DMV were just so he could end up with that particular plate number. Coincidence?

A few months went quickly by. On January 4, 2008, Tom received a disturbing phone call from Carol. The nursing home had just called her, saying that Elinor had apparently suffered a slight stroke. The on-duty nurse was asking what to do, presumably because of her DNR order.

Upset, Tom told his sister to call them right back and demand to know what *they* are going to do! Does she need to go to the hospital or what?

About twenty minutes went by, and Carol called back, sobbing deeply, barely able to speak. "Mom's dead!" she cried.

A couple days later, Tom arrived in Illinois for the funeral. As they were preparing for the eulogy, the family was approached by a woman asking if she could say a few words to the family. Carol knew who she was and said yes, so she went to the podium. The woman explained to the audience that she was the on-duty nurse who was with Elinor in her last moments. She described the following:

After receiving the phone call back from Carol, she decided to call an ambulance.

The nurse said, "Elinor, we're going to call an ambulance to take you to the hospital."

The nurse reached out and placed her hand on the phone. At that same moment, Elinor reached over and placed her hand on the nurse's. Elinor's hands were usually very shaky, and her voice weak, but not this time.

Firm and steady, she gently squeezed the nurse's hand and spoke in a clear voice, "Don't call the ambulance. We don't need them."

She turned her head to look up, pointed to the ceiling, and said, "Look up there. They're coming for me."

Her arms dropped, and she died. The nurse sat there in a long moment of reverence, head bowed, not daring to look up, as she felt an overwhelming sense of awe with what had just happened.

TOM

Tom's turn came to say a few words about his mother. He shared the story about his mom's favorite Bible verse, her letters, and held his license plate in hand for all to see: RC 828.

In Tom's owns words, "That's another one of those amazing things. There is a god. He loves us, and I'm not worthy of all he's done for me. I have great kids, who all have a great life. We've all been blessed. I've had everything I ever wanted, except a hug from my dad. I never got that. My kids hug me though!"

Chapter Nineteen

The Golden Years

Tom was approaching sixty-seven years old in May of 2013. At that time, he was near the end of a long career in pest control. For nearly forty years, Tom had labored at building a very successful business. It had gone by a few different names over the years, like TC Pest Control, General Lawn, Coryell and Sons, or simply Coryell Pest Control. By any name, it was a highly recognized brand in Tom's region, simply because of the quality work he did. His reputation was top-notch. His customers knew it, and so did his competitors.

The Terminix Corporation had approached him several times over the previous couple of years expressing an interest in purchasing Tom's business. Tom had done quite well with the business, averaging nearly six figures annually over the previous decade or so. His success had enabled him to acquire a large tract of land, on which he built a custom home, a large outbuilding, cattle, and various equipment and tools to run the farm and the pest control business. The business was still doing very well when Terminix started to pursue him, so he saw no reason to sell. He declined their offers over and over. They simply weren't offering him enough, and he just wasn't ready to retire.

On a particular day that May, Tom woke up with the sunrise like he always did to start his day. His wife, Judy, was out of town in Kentucky with her father, whose health was failing. Tom was there on the Kansas farm all alone. His usual routine was to place his phone on the kitchen counter and then sit down at the dining room table for coffee and breakfast. But on this day, Judy wasn't home, so he could enjoy his meal on the couch! He set his coffee and breakfast on the coffee table and laid his phone beside him on the sofa.

He finished his breakfast and sat there watching the morning news. He reached for his coffee cup, when out of nowhere, an immense explosion of pain filled his chest and arms. It was a massive heart attack. Gasping for breath and barely able to move, he slumped over.

The thought ran through his mind, *I'm dying! This is what killed my dad!*

In that moment, he felt something under his elbow. It was the cell phone that should have been over on the kitchen counter.

Tom says, "Had I not done that, I'd be dead today."

He struggled to wiggle his elbow just enough to get the phone out from underneath him. With his other arm dangling near the phone, his vision fading fast, he managed to get into his contacts list of over a hundred numbers and pressed the first one that came up; amazingly, it was Mercy Hospital. Many excruciating minutes rolled by as he lay there helplessly on the phone with emergency services. He was finding it more and more difficult to stay conscious as the ambulance raced across the many miles to his rural Kansas property. His strength was fading. He was calling out to God. If he could just hang on a little longer . . .

To the astonishment of the EMT crew, the ER staff, to his doctor, to the heart surgeon, and to all who have heard the tale, Tom survived the almost-two hours that passed from the initial heart attack to being stabilized at the hospital seventy-five miles away. The news finally came to Tom that night as he rested, plugged in to several machines that were keeping him alive. Tom's arteries had over 90 percent blockage. Open-heart surgery would be required as soon as possible and would involve multiple bypasses.

Fear, doubt, regret, a hundred emotions flowed through Tom. Is this his life's last chapter? Surely not. Will he survive the surgery? Will he even make it through the night? What will this mean for his business and the farm? Will he be seeing Danny soon? Dear God.

Morning came, and he woke up. He then survived a twelve-hour, septuplet bypass procedure. That is seven bypasses! All those years of physical labor running his pest control business and keeping up his property had apparently paid great dividends in strength and stamina; now for recovery.

Three or four weeks later, the reality of his situation pressed down hard. June was the most critical month of the year for his business. If he didn't get his quarterlies done, it could ruin him.

What am I going to do? he thought to himself.

It took every ounce of strength he had, holding on with both hands, to even sit upright at the table. He couldn't even feed himself. How in the world is he going to run a business and keep up the property?

In the midst of all that anxiety, Tom bowed his head to pray, "Lord, what do you want me to do? I can't work. I'm going to lose everything I've worked my whole life for. You've blessed me. Now, I need your help."

Long minutes ticked by as he sat there pondering his dilemma, staring out the window across his little piece of the Kansas prairie he had named Serendipity. The phone rang. Tom answered, and it was Terminix! The very same man with whom he had spoken at least half a dozen times about selling his business. He wanted to come out with a couple of his associates and talk to Tom again about selling. Nearly speechless at what he was hearing, Tom could hardly believe God would work so fast!

"Well, sure, yeah. Come on out," Tom replied.

Arrangements were made for the meeting. The group came out to Tom's home, and they sat down at the kitchen table with Tom and Judy. The man could plainly see that Tom was not doing well, so Tom told them about his heart surgery.

Tom recalls, "I really thought they had me over a barrel. I was worried they would try to lowball me and take advantage of my situation."

They reaffirmed their strong interest in Tom's business and that it was exactly what they were looking for to expand into that market region. They expressed a genuine appreciation for his reputation and commitment to customer satisfaction. They reviewed his records, confirming what they already knew was a very profitable business. It was going to be a great win for them if they could just make the right offer to Tom. The man spoke a number. Tom felt a surge of excitement, knowing full well that it was an amazing offer!

He glanced over at Judy to read a very clear message in her eyes, "Oh dear God, don't you dare turn that down!"

He reached up, rubbed his chin, and was just about to open his mouth to say it was a good offer and to accept.

The man blurted out, "Before you turn me down, Coryell, I've been authorized to offer you a monthly check on top of that, for the next five years."

What a miracle! An absolute godsend! Tom accepted, of course.

Tom still had a long road of recovery ahead of him, and there was no way he could maintain an eighty-acre place in his condition. Serendipity was put on the market. In two weeks, he had an offer, and in four weeks, it was sold! They came out way ahead on it too, making a significant gain on their original purchase price. Their retirement was secure! Praise the Lord!

As these life-altering events fell into place, Tom couldn't help but recall a strange encounter he had barely a year before. It was in the fall of 2012 when he was visiting a local church. A guest speaker was there that day, a man Tom had never met or seen. In the minutes before the service began, as people were filing in, visiting with one another, Tom was seated and greeting folks passing by. The guest speaker casually strolled by on his way to the front when he turned his head and locked eyes with Tom. The man stopped in his tracks, looked upon Tom with a piercing gaze, and spoke.

"Your life is going to change in a big way in 2013. You're going to do something big," he said.

He turned and continued walking to the front and sat down like nothing had happened. Stunned, Tom just sat there, wondering. He knew in his heart that was a prophetic moment. Just like Tom had seen various visions of people over the years, he knew that man had just seen something in him in that moment.

Sitting in his home a year later recovering from heart surgery, having just departed with his life's work, the premonition had come true. Tom's life had indeed changed in a big way in 2013, and he was well on his way to a whole new life chapter.

A strange series of complications came up that delayed the transfer process with Terminix. Similarly, unusual twists and turns happened with finalizing the sale of Serendipity. At one point, the property buyers had completely backed out of the deal, and the place went back on the market. As those events dragged on, Tom spent many hours researching places to retire. He was leaning toward Texas, but Judy was leaning toward Tennessee. Tom waffled back and forth—Texas or Tennessee? He had enjoyed many wonderful Texas hunts over the years and was hooked. Judy had family in Tennessee, and her parents were just a few hours from there in Kentucky. He considered other locations too, including Arkansas, Florida, Kentucky, and Arizona.

Something was happening during that time that had a strong influence on Tom's decision. It was the situation with Judy's father. She spent much of her time away tending to that situation while Tom handled affairs back in Kansas. The drive was over ten hours, while from Tennessee, it would only be about three or four. It would be a central and convenient location. Tom was beginning to lean toward Tennessee.

Another event was unfolding that also had some influence on Tom. His oldest son, Steve, had been considering a change in venue for some time. He had recently gone through a difficult divorce and wanted to leave the Kansas City area, but something was holding him back. It was "that thing in her head." The one that Tom had dreamed about years before. Isabelle was dying.

Since 2005, Isabelle had slowly declined, and by that time in late 2013, she was near the end of her eight-year struggle. Steve was watching and waiting for the dreadful day to be behind him before he would be ready to move away. Steve and his new wife, Cheri, had already formed a pretty good idea of where they wanted to be. As a traveling consultant, his job had taken him to various places over the years. In 2012, one of those places was none other than Nashville,

TOM

Tennessee. Steve fell in love with the area right away, traveling once a month to the south suburbs of Franklin and Brentwood. Being a country music superfan, and more than ready for a change of her own, Cheri was on board. But there was still some uncertainty in Steve's heart. "Where is Dad going?"

At approximately 10:00 a.m., on October 30, 2013, Tom sat down at his kitchen table with the Terminix people for the last time to execute the final signatures on the sale of his business. His life's work was over. The check was in hand. Coryell Pest Control was no more. By 6:00 p.m. that very same day, Isabelle was gone.

Tom says, "The one woman who said I was a workaholic and had no time for her . . . she passed away on the same day I sold my business. I don't know how to explain it. Is it just a coincidence? I don't think so."

That was a surreal moment for Tom, realizing how those two life events had just intersected. There was a strange irony with it, where, as Tom's work kept him away from Isabelle, now that his work was gone, so was she. Perhaps this final "coincidental" event was what Tom needed to fully let go of the hurt from how badly things ended with his first wife. Maybe it was the finality that comes with death that gave him the closure he needed to finally close that chapter of his life for good. Whatever the reason is, Tom is convinced that there is a clear and divine purpose behind it. Deep meaning. Full-circle stuff.

A couple months later, Tom was dealing with a nagging recovery issue. The wire sutures in his sternum from the bypass surgery never healed properly and had become infected. He needed to go in for an outpatient procedure to have a rough edge of one of the wires clipped off because it was preventing the healing process.

Judy was away in Kentucky again with her dad. The end was getting close for that situation, so Tom made arrangements for his son Steve to drive him to the hospital and back. Some nasty winter weather was moving in on the day of the procedure, laying down a sheet of ice, sleet, and snow. Steve managed to get his dad back home safely. As Tom got settled into his chair and drifted off to sleep, Steve anxiously waited for his wife, Cheri, to traverse the dangerous conditions. She finally made it, and they spent the next couple of days riding out the storm at Serendipity looking after Tom.

On one of those days, Tom sat at the kitchen table and continued with his investigative work into where his next home would be. He flipped through his handwritten notes, reviewed the things he liked and disliked, and brought up the listings on his computer to look at pictures. He was clearly still undecided. His selection of listings included locations in Texas, Arkansas, Southern Missouri, and Tennessee. Tom paused and stared out the window at the falling snow, wondering what to do.

Steve and Cheri joined him at the table. He began to talk about his options and the deciding factors. It became quite evident that Tennessee was leading the pack. There were several Tennessee homes at the top of his list. Besides being the most affordable state for him, the positives that Tennessee offered to Judy for her dad's situation were clear. Tom was definitely leaning toward Tennessee. Steve and Cheri looked at each other across the table with a grin thinking the same thing, *Looks like we're going to Nashville.*

It didn't take long for that to be confirmed because Judy's father passed away on December 28, 2013. She wanted to be close to her mother, so they decided on Tennessee. A couple months later, Tom and Judy took a trip to Murfreesboro, Tennessee, to visit her brother Joel and begin their house hunt.

Tom says, "We started over on the east side, and when we drove up over those Smokey Mountains, I said to myself, 'We're never leaving here!' I didn't know Tennessee was that pretty!"

The more they went out to explore the countryside looking at properties, the more he was convinced that Tennessee was a perfect fit. If there was any doubt left in Tom's mind, the next thing to happen was his final convincer.

He received a phone call from Steve, who told him he was moving to—you guessed it—Murfreesboro, Tennessee! The very same town they were staying in, and within an hour or two of the places they had been looking at!

TOM

Steve and Cheri moved to Murfreesboro on May 1, 2014. One month later, Tom and Judy moved into a country home near the small town of Morrison, about an hour's drive south of Murfreesboro.

In his seventies now, and fully recovered from his heart surgery, Tom hits golf balls just about every day, shoots his bow and arrow, goes fishing, shoots his guns, hunts deer, and has even acquired a job at the local Walmart. Tom is showing few signs of the retired life, keeping himself busy in his golden years, and now writing this book about his blessed life. Looking back at how those intertwined 2013 events unfolded, it is evident that they were divinely inspired. God is still at work guiding Tom's life. As they say, timing is everything. It was essential for all those things to fall into place, on God's timeline—RC 828.

CHAPTER TWENTY

Still at Work

GOD'S WORK KNOWS no age. That is evident in the many stories that can be found in the Bible where old folks and young folks alike are used by God to accomplish great things. From Daniel to Abraham, Mary and Sara, age clearly doesn't matter to God. Likewise, after seventy-plus years, Tom's gift of dream vision is still at work.

In 2016, Tom's youngest son, Tom Jr., was nearing the end of his maritime studies at the University of Texas A&M in Galveston. He had been working through the very difficult program to earn his credentials as a US Merchant Marine. The final set of certification tests to achieve that honor are brutally comprehensive. Tom Jr. was feeling the pressure, exhausted from hours, weeks, and months of preparation leading up to the test. So much so, that when a particularly unscrupulous individual approached him with an enticing offer, Tom Jr. actually considered it. Certain information could be acquired, for the right price, that could give him an incredible advantage on the final tests. In other words, he could cheat.

Tom Sr. was abruptly awakened one night around this time. Sweating, upset, and 4:00 a.m., he sat there wondering what the heck was going on with his son to have such a disturbing dream about him.

Tom describes the dream as follows, "I was in a strange place sitting on a sofa. I had no control over what was happening in this house, but Tommy was there. He was across the room talking to some people that he apparently knew pretty well. I couldn't make out what they were saying, but I could tell it wasn't going well. One of the guys he was talking to became very upset and pulled out a gun. I just sat there and watched, unable to move. The guy pointed it right at Tommy and killed him! Shot him right in the head!"

It should be no surprise that Tom could not shake that dream vision. After all, he had already seen a son die in a dream and watched it come true. He called Tommy as soon as he could. The conversation went something like this:

> Tom Sr.: "Is there someone you know in your life who would ever try to hurt you?"
>
> Tom Jr.: "Umm, maybe. Why? What's going on, Dad?"
>
> Tom Sr.: "Well, I saw him kill you in a dream. I don't know what's going on, Tom. Maybe you'd like to enlighten me or tell me it was just a dream, son?"
>
> Tom Jr. (a long moment of silence and a heavy sigh): "Yes, Dad. Something is going on."

Tom Jr. divulged to his father that he was tempted to follow through on a deal to get information for cheating on his tests. Tom Sr. urged him to not do it. He was convinced that the dream was a warning message about it all. It may not have meant the literal end of his life, but it could very well mean the death of Tommy's education and career as a Merchant Marine. Tom Jr. agreed and did not cheat. He doubled down on his exam preparations and is proud and certified member of the US Merchant Marines.

Chapter Twenty-One

Full Circle Moments

THIS IS THE part of Tom's book where he finds himself looking back on certain moments in time when a nugget of truth was revealed—a "full-circle moment," when Tom realized just how meaningful a particular encounter truly was.

Full Circle with Steve

Let's start with Steve's story. If you recall, Tom and Steve were the best of friends in the late 1960s sharing a love of hunting and archery in Minnesota and Wisconsin. In 1976, Tom was living in Oak Grove, Missouri. He had just recently moved into town from his unsuccessful venture with Rockwood Acres and was beginning to build his start-up business, TC Pest Control. He received a phone call one evening from an old friend back in Red Wing, Minnesota. It was Dolores, with whom he had worked at Riviera Kitchens and spent so much time with her husband, Fred, out in the Wisconsin woods hunting.

Dolores was calling with some very sad news. Her nephew was killed in a hang gliding accident; it was Steve. Tom's heart sank. Oh no. His dear friend. Tom's mind went immediately back to 1968, when he saw his buddy for the last time standing on the hill by the church, still unsaved.

Dolores told Tom about the success Steve had been enjoying performing professional stunts in his motor-propelled hang glider. He had a manager named Doc and a whole crew for those gigs. In fact, he was conducting an action sequence, practicing for an upcoming movie scene, when the accident happened. He had just completed another practice run and was heading back to the platform when the motor died. The strange sequence of events that unfolded in the seconds that followed baffled all who witnessed it.

Steve was well within the distance needed to simply glide in and land safely on the platform, but something possessed him to reach back and pull on the motor crank to restart the engine. When he did that, the glider flipped over hard. His restraints were snapped, and he was flipped upward into the air away from the glider. He plummeted 350 feet straight down onto the rocks below and was killed instantly.

A few days later, Tom was standing in a Minnesota funeral home looking at his friend's closed casket with a picture on top of how he had remembered his hunting buddy. A man came up and introduced himself. It was Doc.

"I don't think we've ever met," Doc said.

Tom reached out and shook Doc's hand. "My name's Tom Coryell."

A strange hush fell across the group of guys standing there.

With a surprised look on his face, Doc responded, "You're Tom Coryell? You're the guy who shot those deer with a bow!"

At that moment, the other guys responded in like manner, amazed that they were actually meeting the Robin Hood of Ellsworth. Apparently, Steve had told that story over and over to all his friends and hang gliding crew until Tom had become some kind of a local legend. After a bit of bantering with everyone about Steve and Tom's famous hunting story, Tom paused and asked Doc if he had seen the accident. The exchange went like this:

> Doc: "I was so close, Tom, it felt like I could have reached out and grabbed him as he fell."

Tom: "What did you see?"

Doc: "He had his feet crossed, and his hands were folded up under his chin, praying. I heard him hollering 'JESUS!' all the way down."

At that moment, Tom finally understood why he had acted so strangely on that day eight years before, yelling at Steve to call on Jesus in the last fleeting seconds of his life, because he quite literally did, and he was saved because of it.

Full Circle with Danny

The next full-circle moment is about Tom's long-lost little boy, Danny. That was such a tragic and terrible accident that ripped apart a young family, but the impact went far deeper than Tom ever knew until this moment.

In May of 2013, Tom lay in his hospital bed recovering from heart surgery. Family and friends came and went, wishing him well, marveling at the miracle of his victory over certain death. Among those folks were several old friends from way back in his Pekin High School days. They had called him on the phone, encouraging him to hang in there. One caller was especially nice to hear from.

Tom says, "Bob was one of my best friends. He only lived a block from me. We grew up together. He called me. I hadn't heard from him in forty-some years. He got hurt in Vietnam, shot three times, and was pretty distant."

The two old friends carried on a long and pleasant conversation catching up with each other and sharing memories from days gone by. One particular memory that came up was, of course, little Danny.

Bob came right out and asked Tom, "Is that why you left Pekin, because of Danny?"

Tom replied, "Yes, it was. I could not stay there anymore. I had to leave."

The conversation continued, and Bob asked Tom if he knew anything about the kid who was driving the car that hit Danny that day.

Bob said the name, but Tom could not recall anything about him, saying, "I did not know him."

Bob then divulged that he had known the teenager. In fact, he and his parents knew the family very well.

Bob said to Tom, "A year . . . one year after you left Pekin and went to Kansas City, he could not live with what had happened, and he killed himself."

Tom's heart sank. "My god. What a horrible tragedy."

Two children died that day. Two families were altered forever. Danny died within a couple days, and the other boy died a year later.

Sometimes Tom still wonders why Danny had to die. But often it is very clear to him. When he recalls all the times he has shared Danny's story, and all the people who have shed tears over the heartbreak of it, he knows that Danny is still touching lives, all these years later, moving the spirit of people toward God's truth.

Tom reflects, "As a young kid in trouble back when Isabelle was pregnant with Danny, I'm glad that abortion was never a thought. Even though we lost him anyway, I can't imagine my life without him in it. I'd never have his amazing story to share. His short life mattered. It still does."

Full Circle with Rockwood Acres

On a lighter note, the next full-circle moment for Tom involves his son Steve. In 2003, Steve had acquired a new home near the small Missouri town of Lone Jack. It wasn't too long after settling in that Steve invited Tom over for a housewarming visit. As the father and son sat outside on the deck visiting, Steve proceeded to tell Tom about a pleasant surprise he had recently experienced.

Steve decided to take a leisurely walk one day to explore an old gravel road that led north into the hills near his new Lone Jack home. As Steve rounded a particular corner and topped a ridge that overlooked a small valley, it was déjà vu. He felt a strange sensation that he had seen that place before. Searching his memory, he couldn't quite place it. Steve continued further on, sloping down the valley and rising back up again to another ridge. With each step up the next hill, the place became more and more familiar. At the moment he crested the ridge to see the valley before him, a flood of memories filled his mind. With a childish grin, Steve knew right away that he was gazing upon the most favorite of all his childhood homes. It was Rockwood Acres.

"Are you kidding me!" exclaimed Tom.

"Nope. You wanna go have a look?" asked Steve.

The two hopped in the truck and drove down the old road. Sure enough, as they crested the hilltop, Tom knew exactly what he was looking at. Before him were the lakes, the gatehouse entry, now marked as Lake Paradise, his old neighbor's family home now a bait shop, and the old dam road leading up to an empty parking lot overlooking the lakes where two mobile homes once stood that Tom had dug over one hundred feet of waterline by hand thirty years before.

They walked along the shore of the lake sharing old memories of catching fish, shooting squirrels, duck hunting, and skipping rocks across the water. As they stood there taking it all in, Tom shared this thought with his son; all those hard hours of labor he had spent working the land was a form of grief therapy for him. With each drop of sweat, every shovel of dirt, and every swing of the pickax, he felt a little bit less of the burden of Danny's loss.

As if to thank an old friend for being there in his time of need, Tom grinned with a certain look of satisfaction as he noticed many of the improvements he had made three decades before were still visible.

Full Circle with Isabelle

Tom was able to realize a few full-circle moments regarding his first wife, Isabelle. Let's start with "that thing in her head." It was between 2004 and 2005 when she had begun to experience some of the early warning signs of the disease that took her life. The symptoms included

- spells of dizziness, sometimes causing her to fall and injure herself;
- reduced motor control, being off balance, and easily dropping things;
- cognitive distress, where memories and thinking were often slow or blank; and
- shaking, in her hands or shoulders, like one might see in a Parkinson's patient.

There were no explanations for Isabelle. She went to doctors, specialists, therapists, allergists—one doctor after another for over a year, and she got no closer to an answer than when she started. Frustrated, she decided to make a pilgrimage north. She had heard about the Mayo Clinic in Rochester, Minnesota. Her youngest son, Tommy, drove her up to the clinic, and she spent the next couple of weeks going through the process of being tested and evaluated by some of the best and brightest minds in health care. Finally, an answer was found. Sadly, the answer was devastating. Incurable, untreatable, the Cerebella Atrophy was only going to get worse and would someday kill her.

Upon his return home, Tommy shared the news with his father. Tom realized in that moment the truth of the strange dream from so many years before. It didn't bring any new answers or revelations to his heart, because the dream had already done that for him. It had inspired him to drive back to Illinois and forgive Isabelle's father in the cemetery that day, releasing many of his unresolved feelings.

Isabelle's condition progressively worsened over the next few years to the point where she could no longer live alone. Confined to a wheelchair, struggling to speak, or to even feed and clothe herself, she moved in with her daughter Becky.

It was during those years when the whole family was gathered together one holiday for a Christmas Eve dinner. It was a rare and special time, where everyone was together, happy, and enjoying each other's company, kind of like a dream Tom once had.

Tom recalls, "Everyone had gone into the next room after eating, and me and Isabelle were the only ones left at the table. She reached out and grabbed my hand. It caught my attention because it was a grab I recognized, one I didn't want to let go of. She held my hand like she meant it and spoke with intention."

Isabelle said, "Tom, I want to apologize for everything I ever did to hurt you. Can you ever forgive me?"

Tom had already forgiven Isabelle many years before that moment. But in his heart, he was elated to actually hear a sincere apology from the woman who had so utterly broke his heart. That was a healing moment—for both of them. Full-circle stuff.

Of course, Isabelle died in October 2013 from her disease. It was a couple months after that when Tom was recovering from a procedure that cleaned up a nagging issue from his heart surgery. You may recall that is when his son Steve had driven him home in an ice storm and was caring for him while Judy was out of town. Tom was finally able to realize a full-circle moment with his son concerning the truth of the events in Oak Grove.

Tom says, "I chose to keep those things to myself all those years because my kids were so close to their mom. I didn't want to affect that. I had already lost everything. My family was gone, my ministry was gone—there was no value in telling the truth. I just wanted to protect my kids. But after Isabelle died, I decided it was time to heal the rest of us so that my kids would no longer have a bad impression of their father."

Tom explained the situation to Steve, how Walter and Ernie had framed him with a lie and how he had to accept it in order to protect his kids from the true nature of Isabelle and Marla's relationship. For the first time, Tom was finally able to tell the truth to his son. As he watched Steve process the revelation, he wasn't quite sure what the reaction would be.

In Steve's own words, "I reeled at the thought. I was floored that he would do that for me, for my sister and brothers . . . to take the shame, the guilt, for something that was totally not his doing . . .

all for the sake of protecting us from the fallout. How he was able to carry that blame for so many years is beyond me. I told my dad he was my hero. It was always such a barrier for me, deeply affecting my relationship with my dad, believing in something about him for my whole life that was a lie. I immediately felt ashamed for harboring so many ill feelings, for so long, about a man that didn't deserve it. And now, I have to resolve my own hurt from it with a person whom I can't . . . my mom is gone. I can't hear her side of the story. I can't ask her why she allowed me to believe those lies about my dad, even after I was grown-up. I can't tell her how much it hurts me . . . kind of like when she buried her dad, I guess, never able to tell him how much he hurt her. I'll be working on this with God for a while."

Full Circle with David

Tom's next full-circle moment is with another one of his sons, David. You remember him. He's the one who got sent away to the Watkins Mill Boys' Home for armed robbery.

Many years after David's run-in with the law, Tom was sitting at the kitchen table one day visiting with his adult son. They were catching up with each other, because David had been away from the area for quite a while. He was working his way through the Spartan College of Aviation in Tulsa, Oklahoma.

Tom was well-pleased with David for pursuing that career path. At one point in his life, Tom had his own dreams of one day becoming a pilot. Tom told him so, beaming with pride for all that David had overcome in his life, especially considering how close he had come to spending many years of it in prison. The conversation went back to those tenuous times, and for the first time, Tom heard the following details about the night David was arrested.

It was August 1988. David had just turned sixteen in May, and Tommy was fourteen as of January that year. They were living in Odessa, Missouri, and their mother, Isabelle, had recently been remarried to a man named Larry. Larry had a few kids of his own, so it was quite a large, blended family, all living together in a modest house in that small Missouri town.

Larry was a foul and harsh man, absorbed with anger and drinking issues. He was abusive to all the kids, but he was especially hard on David, Tommy, and on his own teenage son Daniel. The crazed man would often sit alone at the kitchen table, sauced up on whiskey, with a loaded .38 revolver on the table just waiting for some trouble to start. The three boys were sick and tired of it, so they began making plans to run away.

During that summer, David had performed some regular work for one of the neighbors, helping out around the man's yard and house to earn some spending money. The man had something in his garage that caught David's attention, something that could help the boys pull off their escape plan. It was a pair of quad runners. When David told Tommy and Daniel about the idea, the imaginations of teenage boys ran wild as they envisioned themselves riding off into the sunset to live free, finding gas and food as they went.

The time had finally arrived to execute their plan. The boys snuck out into the night, armed with Larry's fully loaded .38 Special. They hijacked their mother's car, loaded it up with their "survival gear," and drove over to the neighbor's house where the quad runners were. They parked a short distance away from the house and sat there for several minutes. The windows began to fog up, so they turned on the defrosters full blast to clear the fog. The plan was for Tommy to wait in the car in case they needed to make a quick getaway, while David and Daniel broke into the garage. They would signal Tommy when they were ready and then drive off together. They shut off the car and slipped out. Tommy moved to the driver's seat as the other two boys made their way to the garage door.

While trying to break in, they made a very loud noise. They knew right away that they had to abort. Surely the homeowner heard the sound. They ran away and hid in the shadows to signal for their getaway. Tommy was just a fourteen-year-old kid and completely inexperienced at operating a vehicle, so he didn't realize that he was supposed to turn the key completely over to engage the starter. He thought the car was ready to go when he turned the key and heard the defrosters blowing, but when he dropped it into gear and pressed the gas, nothing happened.

Panic began to set in. Tommy had no idea why the car wouldn't go. He started to push buttons and flip levers. The headlights came on and shined directly upon David and Daniel. They frantically waved their arms, motioning for Tommy to turn off the damn lights! Then the high beams came on! David and Daniel ran to the car.

As they stood there by the driver's door asking Tommy what the heck was he was doing, a man's voice spoke loudly from behind them, "Hold it right there, boys! The police are on their way."

The boys slowly turned around. A barely visible figure stood before them, just a few feet away. Frozen with fear, unsure what to do, the two boys stared in silence at the back-lit silhouette.

David heard a faint whisper from Daniel, "The gun—use the gun to scare him off."

David's heart was pounding, his nerves were trembling, he felt the revolver in his pocket.

"Do it!" urged Daniel.

David reached into his pocket, pulled out the gun, pointed it at the man, and pulled back the hammer. The man reacted instantly, throwing up his hands and grunting with the sound of a fierce animal. He immediately ducked into the shadows. David caught a split-second glimpse of something in the man's hand that looked an awful lot like a gun just before he disappeared from sight.

From the darkness came a loud command, "Put it down, son! Put it down, or I'll kill you! I *will* kill you!"

David complied. He laid the revolver on the ground, put his hands up, and began apologizing profusely. The police arrived within minutes and arrested the three boys.

As Tom sat at the table with David all those years later, listening to that tale, his eyes widened, and his face took on a shocked look. He stood up and paced the floor, shaking his head in disbelief as he made the mental connection; at the very same moment David stood there in the darkness that night with a gun pointed at him, Tom was standing outside on Twila's deck seventy miles away praying for his kids' very lives.

Full Circle with Tom's Salvation

The next full-circle moment for Tom spans nearly fifty years, going back to a time when he was just a young teenager in Illinois. At age sixty-something, about 2008, Tom was living a pretty good life on his Kansas farm running the pest control business. His kids were all grown, had families of their own, and he was at a point in his life of looking back at the long road of life he had traveled.

Tom recalls, "After Danny's death, the divorce, and all that had happened, I wanted to believe that I had lived a good life. But I didn't feel that way. I did some pretty bad things in the eighties, things I was ashamed of."

Tom was feeling a sense of guilt, wrestling with the behavior of days past when he was a prodigal after the divorce and acting out in the worst of ways. As he sat on his sofa one day trying not to dwell on those feelings, he focused on preparing his daily work schedule. Something on the television caught his attention. On the screen was "Billy Grahm Crusades—1962—McCormick's Building—Chicago, IL."

Tom remembers the moment, "It was like something hit me over the head! I got goose bumps and couldn't believe it! I was there! In 1962, at that very meeting!"

Obviously, Tom's attention promptly abandoned his work schedule preparations, and he focused on the TV. He excitedly called his sister Carol, and they both watched together trying to find themselves in the grainy old black-and-white video. Sure enough, when the end of the sermon came and the invitation was made, Tom watched the image of his sixteen-year-old self make his way down to the front where he prayed the sinner's prayer and accepted Christ for the first time almost fifty years before. A soft, reassuring voice spoke into Tom's sixty-something soul in that moment, confirming something for Tom, "It is well. It is well with my soul."

Tom would be the first to tell you that accepting Christ and believing in his grace and mercy would never be an expectation for a trouble-free life, but he would say that you'd better have God in your life if you ever expect to get through all the stuff that the enemy will throw at you. Going forward on that day in 1962 with Billy Grahm turned out to be the best decision he ever made, and it was nothing short of a miracle to be reminded of that pivotal moment almost fifty years later when he was in a moment of personal guilt and doubt. God never leaves us, even when we leave him, and his forgiveness transcends all trespasses, no matter how deplorable we believe them to be.

Full Circle with the Oak Grove Church

Some people might refer to the next full-circle moment as karma, because it wasn't very many years after the disturbing events at the Oak Grove Church where Ernie and Walter had forced a lie upon Tom, that Ernie was exposed as a hypocrite.

Ernie was caught having an affair with a secretary at his own church. He was a recognized radio personality in the local Kansas City market at that time, but when the truth came out about his infidelity, he lost everything—his wife, his position, his credibility.

Tom recalls with a sense of outrage, "Remember the Bible, Ernie! Judge not lest ye be judged!"

With a slight chuckle, Tom muses, "Boy. How true."

Regarding Walter, Tom says, "He lost that church. A church that started out with only six families and grew to over 550 people is now a just a flea market. A broken-down old building. Walter's wife passed away, and he spent the rest of his life, not as a pastor, but as a carpenter building churches."

Tom had plenty of years after those ugly events in Oak Grove to try and understand what drove Walter to despise him so much. It finally dawned on him many years later. He shared the following story.

A particular woman named Mary came to the church one day. She liked what she saw and decided to attend regularly. However, she always came alone. Her husband refused to go. Tom noticed this, so he went out to their home several times and came to know Mary's husband. He smoked like a chimney, drank like a fish, and cussed like a sailor. He was one who felt like he didn't need church to know God. He could find God in the woods or in his backyard. Tom developed a pretty good rapport with the man.

It wasn't the first time he had to break through such a tough exterior, remembering his days with Odie back at Caterpillar, or Bill from Riviera Kitchens. That was a distinct difference in Tom's style versus Walter's. Tom was hands-on, in person. He witnessed, shared his testimony, and he led people openly and verbally in reciting the sinner's prayer. That is what drew people to him instead of Walter.

Tom recalls, "He didn't know how to lead anybody to Christ. He would always say 'God is good. Isn't God good?' It's like he believed all you had to do was come to church, and you'd be saved. But I know that salvation is a verbal thing. The Bible says so in Romans 10:9, 'If thou shalt confess with thy mouth and believe in thine heart that He is raised him from the dead, thou shalt be saved.'"

Tom received a phone call one day from Mary. Her husband was in the hospital. He had cancer and was dying. She told Tom that her husband was asking if he would come to see him.

Tom replied, "Okay, Mary. I'd be glad to. Let me call Walter, and we'll come up there together."

Mary quickly responded, "No, Tom. Don't bring Walter. He wants to talk to you alone."

Tom agreed. He went to the hospital, knelt with the man, held his hand, and shared the salvation story. With tears filling his eyes, he prayed the sinner's prayer with Tom.

When they finished the prayer, the man looked up into heaven and said, "I felt that. I know now for the first time in my life that I'm saved. I am saved."

Mary's husband died that very night. When word got out about what had happened, Walter was furious. He confronted Tom, chastising him for doing Walter's job. It wasn't very long after that when the rest of those sad events unfolded around Tom.

Another disturbing event occurred around that time, shortly after Mary's husband died. Tom had learned that a particular woman in the congregation was going through a significant bout of depression. It was so severe that it had reached suicidal proportions. On a particular night, the woman had reached out to Walter asking for Tom's phone number. She knew Tom well and was quite comfortable speaking with him about her issues. But Walter refused. He outright denied her request to speak with Tom and forced her to deal with him instead. She took her own life that same night.

Tom's conclusion is that Walter's pride was injured by the fact that he had no ability to lead people to Christ when Tom did. That was evident by how the congregation flocked to Tom, not Walter. It was the beginning of the end for both of them.

In Tom's own words, "The whole thing fell apart. When I walked out of that church, so did the Spirit of God. When I left under those conditions—lies, cheating, anger, animosity, jealousy—to have it all swept under the rug like that, you can't expect God to bless you. It didn't take long after I left for that church to fall apart and die. Ernie's dead. Walter was never a pastor again. But I'm still witnessing and helping people find Christ. In fact, I'm working on some folks even now at my Walmart job. But that's another story."

For over a year, Tom endured the disgrace that Walter and Ernie had put on him. Despite being completely disavowed, shunned, and exiled by the church people he thought cared about him, he continued to make an effort to deal with the Marla and Isabelle's affair. He reached out to Pastor Andrew at the Assembly of God Church and was welcomed by that man. Andrew knew the truth. He knew Tom was a good man. He allowed Tom to give his testimony to the congregation from time to time, to contribute his musical talents playing piano, and even brought Tom into the leadership fold.

It was like déjà vu for Tom. In that one year's time, he watched the small Assembly of God Church grow well beyond the capacity of their little seventy-five-person building.

Tom recalls, "That church packed out. I think a lot of people that knew me from Walter's church started coming to Andrew's. I saw a lot of familiar faces in the pews."

That much growth prompted the leaders to arrange an urgent meeting. It was clear they had outgrown their facility and needed a plan. It just so happened that a recent addition to the team had some experience with rapid church growth—it was Tom. Pastor Andrew invited him to join them in their upper room, a quaint little meeting place elevated behind the pulpit center stage wall overlooking the sanctuary. The discussion swirled, back and forth:

- Should we add on?
- Is there even any room on the lot to expand?
- Should we build a new church?
- Where could we get the land?
- How much land do we need?
- One man mentioned a three-to-five-acre lot nearby ready to go, but can we even afford it?

After much debate, the elders and financial managers chimed in and said there was simply no budget to do any of it. The only thing to do is to start saving money and raise the funds over time. The group paused with a collective sigh, and the room fell silent for a few awkward moments.

Pastor Andrew locked eyes with Tom and said, "Well, Tom, what do you think?"

Tom already knew the answer, because he had lived it his whole life.

He responded, "Are we not a church? Do we not have faith? If we are to preach faith, we must live by faith. God did not intend for the church to come up with the money and then build a church. I believe we should step out on faith, run toward building a church, and let God do the rest."

Long story short, they agreed with Tom. They went out and bought the three to five acres, and the money came in. It wasn't long before a beautiful new church building was erected on that land.

As you know from reading this book, Tom left that area after his divorce with Isabelle. He always wondered what had become of Andrew's church; so many years later when he was living in Kansas, he decided to make the long drive to Oak Grove one Sunday morning to see for himself.

When he arrived, he could hardly believe his eyes. The original structure had grown to include five new additions supporting a capacity of over one thousand people. He walked into the sanctuary to take it all in and found himself a spot near the front.

In his own words, Tom recalls, "I have never seen a more powerful ministry. The church was packed with people. The quality of the music was way beyond anything we ever had back in my day. The church was alive. I could just feel it. I sat there and cried a little, deeply moved by what God had done there."

When the service was over, and everyone stood up to greet one another and file out, Tom turned around to see the very man who had spoken up years ago in the upper room, telling them about the three to five acres. He saw Tom and immediately recognized him. With a huge smile, the two grasped each other's hand with a happy greeting.

"Looks like we made the right decision that day in the upper room, didn't we?" Tom said.

"We sure did," replied the man.

Conclusion

WHAT ARE YOUR full-circle moments? Whose lives have you touched? Who has touched your life? What are the incredible "coincidences" that make you shake your head and wonder if they were divinely arranged?

To make it even more personal, when were your moments with God where he reminded you he is still there? What was your best day, or your worst, where God showed up?

For Tom, there were many. He looks back at his amazing life through the twenty-twenty lens of hindsight and realizes that bad things happen when you just don't care anymore. But it is in those moments when God cares most, waiting for you to see and hear his presence in your life.

This world is full of such stories. Every day God is at work making our lives count and to serve a purpose to those around us. And we may not even know it until fifty years into our future.

For Tom, he feels blessed to have been given such a great life and so many amazing opportunities to use his gifts for God's good work. Now, with a book that chronicles the ways in which he knows God has used him, he hopes and prays that people who read it will be inspired and find great hope in his mother's favorite scripture:

> And we know that all things work together for good to them that love God, to them who are the called according to his purpose. (Romans 8:28, KJV)

Epilogue

A Son's Perspective

It has been an incredible honor and a special treat for me to help my dad with his book. I imagine most sons never had an opportunity like this to know so many intimate details of their father's life story. My dad certainly never knew half as much about his father as I have learned of my own. The journey has been quite a ride, spanning a lifetime of thoughts and feelings. For that, I am grateful, humbled, and I lift up my thanks not only to my dad, but to God.

In my teenage years following my mom and dad's divorce, I convinced myself that I was going to do it better. I formulated a vision in my mind of how my life was going to be as the husband and father my dad never was. That was rather naive of me. Not only because I lacked life experience, but because I lacked the truth.

Looking back through the lens of a grown man with his own life story, and now aware of so many revelations in this book, I'd like to share this son's perspectives.

I was very young when my big brother Danny was killed, not even two years old. I have no memory of him. I grew up with an abstract idea of him based solely upon a picture of him and me that has hung on the wall for almost fifty years. We didn't talk about him. Mom and Dad simply acknowledged who he was and that he was run over by a car a long time ago. As an adult, I asked both my parents about Danny a few times over the years. I managed to collect a few bits and pieces, but the conversation always ended quickly. The topic was very upsetting to both of them, so I never pushed it. It wasn't until 2016 when Dad decided to write this book that I finally heard the whole story.

As you can imagine, it was profound for me. I experienced some full-circle stuff of my own. It gave me some insight into a few of my own behaviors and character traits. For example, I am a highly introverted person. Not antisocial, but certainly one who gravitates toward solitude. My mom used to tease me for spending so much time alone in my room, drawing, reading, or listening to music.

"There goes Steve up to his sanctum sanatorium," she used to joke.

As an older man, I have tried to analyze that. Why am I that way? I think the answer lies in those initial formative years of my life after Danny passed away. The old photos from those days show me and Danny playing together all the time. Our brotherly bonds were solid. It is clear that he and I were inseparable, until . . .

My best friend and playmate simply vanished. My parents sank into grief and despair and were simply out of my reach emotionally for nearly three years. I was too young to understand. This all happened during my most impressionable years, age two to five. I had to adapt to the isolation, and as a result, it became an engrained personality trait in me.

Although I have no memory of Danny, it is rather interesting to know that I have a mental trigger about him. It is a smell. The unique odor of a dirty window screen. Why is it that thoughts of Danny flood my mind every time a cool summer rain falls upon hot asphalt? That aroma is very similar to the smell of a dirty window screen. I think the answer is that, because I was just a toddler, I was not always allowed to go outside with him. So whenever he went outside without me, I would stand at the front door watching him play, breathing in the smell of the screen door wanting badly to be out there with him.

That is only a theory, because I have no true memories of Danny, none that I can recall anyway. I often wonder if I have suppressed memory. Some people have clear memories of their toddler years. I was about nineteen months old when the accident happened, so it is plausible to think that I could have remembered some things from that time. I have a few vague and spotty images in my mind from my grandparents' house (Isabelle's mom and dad), Flossie and Elinor at the old nursing home on Park Avenue, playing with my little sister Becky, or when baby David came home. But my first truly clear memory is of me and my dad riding in a U-Haul truck together bound for Kansas City in 1972.

Something my mother once told me came flooding back to my mind when Dad told me the details about the car that hit Danny. As a young father in the early 1990s, I remember a moment with my mom at her little apartment in Kansas City. My son was a toddler at that time, and he was just beginning to put sentences together. I asked her if she remembered what my first full sentence was. Her reaction was a bit strange. She slowly exhaled a puff of her cigarette and looked deeply into my eyes, pausing for a few moments.

In a rather flat and serious tone, she said, "I'm gonna get that white car."

At the time, it made no sense to me. Maybe I had my eye on a particular toy? But maybe, just maybe, I was talking about that white car that ran over my brother. Could it be that as I stood there at the front door with my little face pressed against the window screen that I watched him run into the street and witnessed the accident firsthand? Is it possible that my mom scooped me up and ran outside to the scene, and while she hysterically witnessed the horror, I was right there in her arms watching the whole thing too? I may never know the truth of that until I meet her again in the afterlife.

That realization prompts another interesting thought about myself. I am a wanderer. I have always had an interest in knowing what lies beyond the horizon, over the next ridge, or around the corner. Even as a little boy, I can remember wandering off, looking for something. I never knew what it was, but I was always slipping away, time and time again. I distinctly remember several times getting a proper butt warming for it too. I have no doubt that I worried my parents sick whenever I did that. They had already lost a son, and they darn sure weren't planning on losing another. Could it be that my wandering behavior was all about looking for that white car? Was I searching for my lost bother? Who knows?

Like any kid who watches their parents' marriage fall apart, it was hard for me. I was thirteen at the time, and I remember clearly when they called us four kids together to break the news. I recall being shocked and surprised. I had no idea it was coming. Caught completely off guard, I quickly ran upstairs to my "sanctum sanatorium" and locked myself away until Dad left.

Looking back from age fifty, having gone through a divorce of my own and now knowing the true backstory of Tom, Isabelle, and Marla, I find myself amazed at how well they shielded us kids from that turmoil. The fact that I was so surprised by the news at age thirteen is a strong testimony for how just much care they took to protect us from the ugly truth. My mom and dad were some awesome people, despite the issues they had.

From my point of view, I have to agree with my dad when he said he missed something important by not knowing what it meant to be a dad. Love and affection was an absent thing for me growing up with him. I rarely ever got a hug or an "I love you" from him. He was physically absent a lot too, working his pest control business and providing for his family. I do have some fond memories with him, however, especially from when we lived at Rockwood Acres. I have vivid memories of hunting and fishing out there. As an older kid, I played tennis and basketball with him. We played video games, and we watched football on TV rooting for Fran Tarkenton and Roger Staubach. There were lots of smiles, laughter, and fun—but no affection.

That is the one area where I hope I did it a little better. I made a conscious effort to be "that father" for my own children. I don't think a day went by that I didn't hold them tight and look into their eyes to intently tell them I loved them. It was my goal to love them in every way that my father was unable to love me. I hope they feel like I nailed it on that one.

Knowing now what I didn't know then, I feel bad for my dad. He was dealt a bad hand and grew up under some very adverse conditions. I am very grateful that he was around for most of my childhood and provided me with a pretty good life. Despite how things turned out with my mom, I am proud to say that he absolutely did do it better than his dad—way better.

I have to give him props for two crucial ideals that he instilled in me growing up. Most importantly, he brought me up under Christian values. Going to church, listening to sermons, singing hymns, attending Sunday school—all those things were an integral part of my childhood up until the divorce. I know who God is because my dad made sure of it. Secondly, the notion of hard work was imprinted upon me at a very young age. I have distinct memories of picking up sticks and raking leaves as young as five years old out at the Rockwood Acres property. I shoveled snow, weeded the garden, mowed the lawn, and dozens of other household chores every day—without an allowance. Laziness and entitlement were never part of the equation for me. Thank you, Dad, for teaching me all about Jesus and hard work. I think those two fit together quite nicely.

In my teenage years after the divorce, I harbored some bad feelings toward my dad. I saw him as a cheater and a philanderer. I believed he was selfish and greedy, unwilling to provide financial support to us. I thought he didn't care enough to even know what was going on in his kids' lives, because I never saw him at any of my football games or track meets.

It was all a lie. He was there. I just didn't know it. He did provide, and he was not the cheater he was made out to be. Even into my adult years, my mother remained silent, allowing me to believe those things about my dad. Reconciling that has been hard for me, because I loved my mother dearly. My heart slowly broke over a period of eight years as I watched her wither away under that horrible disease. I never did hear her side of the story. She simply didn't talk about it. Even when I asked her directly, she refused to divulge any details. She was a very private person.

It was during my thirties that I began to take some personal steps toward healing my relationship with my father. Even without the knowledge I have today from his book, I had reached a place of maturity where I knew it was time to mend those fences. He and I came a long way through the decade of 2000–2010. I grew to love him and to forgive him, despite not having the whole story. I believe that was God's handiwork. Looking back, I am once again floored at the notion of him keeping quiet about the truth of Oak Grove. I forgave him for things that never happened, and he still made no defense. I can hardly process that. My dad is a hero.

I still love my mother deeply. I always will. Knowing the truth of how things went down won't change that. I only wish I could talk to her about it, to understand her heart. I wish I could write her story too. I can't imagine how deep the hurts ran inside of her—abused by her father, burying her firstborn. I caught glimpses of the pain a few times over the years whenever I tried to talk to her about Danny. It was soul crushing every time. And regarding her dad . . . I will never know. What that does to a woman will always be far beyond the realm of understanding for anyone who hasn't been through it themselves, especially for men.

In my view, her story is one of victory. In the early 1990's she surrendered her pain to the Cross and turned from her prodigal ways. She recommitted her heart and life to God, joined a church, and was baptized. The enemy may have won a few battles, but with Jesus, she won the war over her sin. In the last years of her life, my mom modeled an amazing attitude for everyone to see as the disease slowly killed her. Never openly bitter, angry, or depressed, she exhibited a level of grace that I could hardly fathom. She thanked God for every day. She smiled, joked, laughed, and remained as positive as anyone I have ever known. She had clearly reconciled her past with God, and she conducted herself in those waning years as a model Christian woman. Faced with daily decline, physical adversity, and certain death, she operated with a joy that defies human logic. Right up to her last moment, she did it right.

I was glad to learn about my dad's younger days and what had happened to his mom and dad. I never knew my grandpa John. Dad told me that he held me once in Pekin, not long before we moved away to Kansas City. Dad never talked about him, and other family who had known him only voiced their disdain for the man. Likewise, I had heard similar family gossip about my grandma Elinor . . . that she was mental and such. Hearing about what really happened to the two of them was eye-opening, and also heartbreaking.

I must admit that I am somewhat jealous of my dad. He has something I never did. I'm going to call it a spiritual antenna. His gift of being in tune with the Spirit is quite remarkable. That is definitely not my gift. I am about as in tune as a block of wood. That is likely by my Creator's design. I'm pretty sure he knows I wouldn't do very well with dreaming about the death of my child before it actually happened. I think my little brother David may have picked up some of my dad's spiritual DNA, but that is another story, which I hope he writes about someday.

In closing, my hope is that people who read my dad's book are inspired to believe deeper. I hope they experience a fuller faith in knowing that God is always at work, even when we can't see it. People and circumstances, dreams and visions, all the things that help God's people through this life journey are real. I want people to embrace the truth that no matter how deep your sins run, you can overcome with God in your heart. I also want people to realize that things are not always as they seem. Be careful about judging your parents' decisions, because you may not have all the facts. The truth that you are operating on may not be what you think it is. If you have doubts, talk to them. And if you are a mother and father who has been keeping a secret that you know could make a difference in someone's relationship with a parent, speak the truth. It is far better to hurt someone with the truth than to kill them with a lie. God bless.

ABOUT THE AUTHOR

Thomas Coryell was born in Pekin, Illinois, and grew up in his grandmother's nursing home, his biological parents absentees. His true and only father always was, and is, Jesus Christ, his rock and salvation.

Printed in the USA
CPSIA information can be obtained
at www.ICGtesting.com
LVHW041945220124
769383LV00002B/257